EGO on LAKE ONTARIO

*the Wall is surrounded by a Ditch. The ....jection of the Rocks, renders the Channel at the Entrance into the **Onondaga River** very Narrow, and our Vessels are generally warp'd from the Lake. into the Bason.*

{ Explanation .
1. *The River Onondaga .*
2. *The Lake Ontario .*

Engraved & Printed by Jacot & Julien Albany

OLD FORTS OF THE GREAT LAKES: SENTINELS IN THE WILDERNESS

OLD FORTS OF THE GREAT LAKES: SENTINELS IN THE WILDERNESS

James P. Barry

Lansing, Michigan

Old Forts of the Great Lakes: Sentinels in the Wilderness
copyright © 1994 by James P. Barry

Portions of this book appeared in somewhat different
form in *American History Illustrated*, *The Great Lakes
Outdoors*, and *Inland Seas*.

PUBLISHER: Sam Speigel/Thunder Bay Press
TYPESETTING AND LAYOUT:: Maureen MacLaughlin Morris
LOGO DESIGN: Lynda A. Bass

2 3 4 5 6 7 8 9   09 08 07 06 05 04 03 02

ISBN   1-882376-05-6

Thunder Bay Press

Lansing, Michigan

Next Page: Fort Howard at Green Bay c. 1840, after
major rebuilding in 1831-35. From Francis de
Castelnau's *Vue et souvenirs de l'Amerique du nord*,
published in Paris, 1842. (Library of Congress LC-
USZ62-5034)

Title Page: Fort Erie, as seen now from outside the
walls. (Photo by the author)

Frontpiece: Fort Oswego. (K. Knapman Collection)

For Anne

Contents

INTRODUCTION

U.S. soldiers in formation, Fort Mackinac, 1882. At left is the post commander's house, in the background a blockhouse, and at right the barracks. Families are watching from the bank. (Mackinac State Historic Parks)

For two centuries the Great Lakes region was a violent one. From the time the French arrived in the early 1600s and allied themselves with some of the Indian nations in their wars against other Indian nations, until at least a generation after the War of 1812, people felt safest when they were in or near fortified places. Forts in the area were not always military posts. The first European establishment on the Great Lakes, the mission of Sainte Marie among the Hurons, had walls to protect it from the Huron Indians' implacable enemies, the Iroquois. And the later trading posts, such as Fort William, were commercial structures so arranged that they also had some defenses.

Missions, trading posts, and military posts were at the outer edge of empire— at first Imperial France and at last such business empires as John Jacob Astor's American Fur Company. All of them were outposts of a church, business, or government based far away. The distance between the early posts on the Lakes and the capitals at Paris or London, when sending messages or bringing in supplies and reinforcements, was greater than any distance on earth today. Even when the bases of power became Washington, New York, and Montreal, the Great Lakes posts were distant and remote.

As late as the 1840s, when construction of a ship canal between Lakes Huron and Superior was being debated in the United States Congress, Henry Clay declared that this would be "a work beyond the remotest settlement in the United States, if not in the moon"—and his opinion prevailed. Little wonder that during earlier years when a region so far from help was so open to violence, the major centers in it were nearly always fortified.

Many different kinds of forts were built around the Great Lakes. The commonest were log block houses and wooden palisades; often they served a purpose for a few years and were then abandoned. Others were works of earth and stone in the European manner. Such structures were much more likely to survive through the centuries.

Interior of Fort Mississauga, looking across the river to the U.S. Fort Niagara, c. 1840. (By now the oldest building in Fort Niagara—built by the French—doubled as a lighthouse, with a navigational lamp mounted above it.) This small British fort at Mississauga Point, completed at the end of the War of 1812, was an artillery emplacement built to guard the northern flank of Fort George, the guns of which did not command the mouth of the Niagara River. Such detached auxiliary batteries were often used in coastal defenses. The only permanent building at Mississauga was the brick tower, seen here at right. But in the early 1820s the much larger Fort George was abandoned and soon deteriorated, while Mississauga was manned intermittently until the Mackenzie rebellion of 1837. It then was refurbished and garrisoned continuously until the 1850s, after which it and the surrounding grounds were used for training camps through World War I. From a watercolor by P.J. Bainbrigge. (National Archives of Canada C11899)

Forts were built at key places. They were the hubs of activity. Because they were important, historical currents swirled in and around them. They saw many of the adventures of France and Britain in the new world, and of the fledgling United States as it first stretched its boundaries.

Their very presence influenced history; the British must seize Fort Niagara in order to wrest America from the French, for example, and when the Americans lost the fort at Detroit they had to build a naval squadron and fight the Battle of Lake Erie before they could recover the fort and move on into Canada.

When some of the places where forts were located grew even more important and the activity even greater over the centuries, the resulting cities at times overwhelmed their parents; Fort Ponchartrain is now lost beneath the paving of Detroit and Fort Dearborn beneath that of Chicago. Others served their purpose and disappeared; the exact location of some of them is still a question. A number of the old forts have survived, however, and others have been reconstructed. Today there are enough of them that one can visit forts of nearly every era and see and feel what life in those days must have been like.

Fort Ontario barracks, built in 1842, housed an average of seventy men on the second floor. The first floor contained a kitchen and a schoolroom. (Fort Ontario State Historic Site).

1
THE FRENCH ON THE GREAT LAKES

In 1610 the first European to reach the Great Lakes, an 18-year-old French youth named Étienne Brûlé, came down French River to Georgian Bay, riding with Huron Indians returning in their canoes from their annual trading visit to Quebec. He spent several years living with the Hurons at the southeastern corner of Georgian Bay and travelling through the rest of the Great Lakes region.

In 1615 Samuel de Champlain, governor of the French colony at Quebec, came to join the Hurons in an expedition against their enemies the Iroquois. Although the Hurons had asked him to come and had promised him that twenty-five hundred warriors would accompany him, in fact they supplied only five hundred. And when the expedition into what today is upstate New York moved against a palisaded village of one of the Iroquois nations, the Onondaga, the Hurons made only an abortive attack and then retreated. Champlain was wounded in the battle; in some pain and considerable disappointment he went back to the Huron country and spent the winter in the villages there.

The more important Huron villages were fortified and were located as defensive positions along the frontier of Huronia where an Iroquois attack would first reach it. According to Champlain, typical fortifications were "wooden palisades in three tiers, interlaced into one another, on top of which they have galleries which they furnish with stones for hurling, and water to extinguish the fire that their enemies might lay against their pali-

The mission of Sainte Marie among the Hurons was the first European establishment on the Great Lakes. It was fortified about 1644. This reconstruction stands on the original location near Midland, Ontario. (Photo by author)

sades." Such a triple palisade, the French leader noted, was about thirty-five feet high.

While he was living in the Huron country, where there were twenty- to thirty-thousand people, Champlain visited other friendly tribes nearby and met representatives of still more; to all of them he explained the advantages of trading with the French. He was accompanied by Father Joseph LeCaron, a Récollet priest, who could not fail to see the opportunities here for religious missions among a settled people unlike so many of the nomadic Indians with whom the French dealt.

In 1623 Récollet missionaries, among them LeCaron, did come. They lived with the Hurons in their villages for a year. In 1626 the first Jesuits arrived. At the same time trade with the French by the Hurons and other friendly nations expanded. Other factors came into play, however. The warlike Iroquois, who traded with the English and Dutch along the Atlantic Coast, had exhausted the fur-bearing animals in their own country; but their enemies, the Hurons, carried canoe loads of pelts to Quebec each year by way of French River, Lake Nipissing, the Ottawa River, and the St. Lawrence River. The Iroquois had only to wait along the canoe route, kill the Huron canoemen, and take their furs.

The Jesuits established a headquarters for their Huron missions in 1639. It was centrally located in Huronia, but away from any village. They called it Sainte Marie. From there the missionaries went out to work in the surrounding villages. They envisioned that it would become the administrative center of a Christian Indian community. In 1642 an Iroquois war party raided Huronia and burned one of the villages. In 1644 twenty-two soldiers from France were sent to Huronia and spent the winter there; probably they built many of the fortifications that surrounded Sainte Marie in its later years. This was the first European center of the Great Lakes, and it became the first fort. (Far to the east, the first small settlements had been established by the Dutch at New Amsterdam in 1626 and the English at Boston in 1630.)

It was a stockaded fort; to this degree it was built in the Indian fashion. But stockades around Indian villages were generally oval in shape; these walls were straight, in the European manner, so that men with muskets could stand in the bastions at the corners of the walls and shoot at any attackers. Several of the bastions were built of stone, a purely European form of construction. One side of the mission fort lay along what is now called the Wye River. The place was a short distance inland from Georgian Bay and the river provided access by the only vehicles there were, canoes. It also gave added protection to that side of the fort. Inside the walls there were dwellings, a chapel, a hospital, carpenter and blacksmith shops, a cookhouse, and other essentials. The structures were built mainly of wood, although there were occasional walls or foundations of stone.

By 1648 continued Iroquois attacks had thrust back the eastern frontier of the Huron country a considerable distance, forcing abandonment of several villages. While this was happening, measles and smallpox, which the French understood little better than the Hurons, were transmitted from the Europeans who had developed some immunity against them to the Indians who had none. A third to a half of the Huron population died, further weakening the nation.

In the spring of 1649 the Iroquois mounted a major attack, destroying two or three more villages and in the process capturing and torturing to death two of the missionaries, Fathers Gabriel Lalemant and Jean de Brébeuf. The Huron nation suddenly collapsed; the Hurons everywhere took fright, burned their remaining villages, and either fled to the protection of friendly tribes in distant places or to Sainte Marie, which the invaders would not attack. But the Indians could not live inside the fort indefinitely, and the Iroquois were certain to return. In May, Father Ragueneau, superior of the mission, and the remaining chiefs agreed that before their enemies came again they should move to the large offshore island today called Christian Island. This they did, burning Sainte Marie behind them so that it would not become an Iroquois stronghold.

Interior of the reconstructed mission of Sainte Marie. (Photo by author)

After a winter of starvation, during which the living were forced to eat the bodies of those who died, the remaining three hundred Christian Hurons decided to go with the missionaries back to the security of Quebec. Huronia was abandoned, both by the Hurons and by the French.

Brûlé in his travels may well have been the first European to see and voyage over Lake Superior, but the first recorded ones to see it were two Jesuit missionaries, Isaac Jogues and Charles Raymbault, who went to Sault Ste. Marie in 1641. When Huronia fell to the Iroquois, however, there was a break in exploration. From 1650, when the Jesuits shepherded the Christian remnant of the Hurons back to Quebec, until 1658 no Frenchmen dared the canoe route to the interior. But in that year two brothers-in-law, Radisson and Groseilliers, once again headed west with a party of Huron and Ottawa Indians. They wintered in southern Wisconsin and the next year probably became the first Europeans to see the upper Mississippi River. They returned to Quebec, but in 1661 came back to the Lakes, travelling as far westward as the Sioux country and probably as far north as Hudson Bay.

Thereafter a stream of French explorers and missionaries spread out through the Great Lakes region, travelling by canoe in summer and on snow shoes in winter. The dispersal of the Hurons and to a lesser degree the Ottawas, who had lived farther north of Georgian Bay, in the long term stimulated the fur trade. These tribes carried French goods to distant places, where other tribes saw and wanted them. French traders followed the dispersed fragments, thus expanding the trade. In 1668 the mission of St. Ignace was established by Father Jacques Marquette on the northern side of the Straits of Mackinac. As the French were able to put more pressure on the Iroquois and reach an uneasy peace with them, they

Plan of Fort Frontenac, 1726, at the present location of Kingston, Ontario. (National Archives of Canada C672)

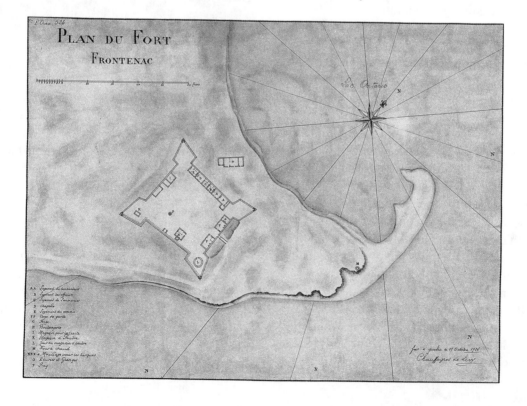

also were able to come directly up the Saint Lawrence River to Lake Ontario and to explore the lower Lakes. In 1669 Louis Jolliet, travelling eastward from Sault Ste. Marie with an Iroquois guide, made the first recorded voyage through Lake Huron, the Saint Clair River, Lake Saint Clair, the Detroit River, and Lake Erie. He then crossed the Niagara Portage and reached Lake Ontario near what later would be the site of Fort Niagara.

The man who was to become perhaps the best-known French explorer, Robert René Cavélier, Sieur de La Salle, travelled over Lake Ontario that same year and probably went as far south as the Ohio River. In June 1671 Saint-Lusson planted a wooden cross at Sault Ste. Marie and proclaimed French sovereignty over the area; in July 1679, at a Sioux village west of Lake Superior, Duluth held a similar ceremony. French exploration was slowed temporarily by another outbreak of war with the Iroquois in 1689, and in that year the French even withdrew for a time from their posts in the West, but in 1690 an expedition of 150 soldiers went out to build Fort Bouade, the first fort on the Straits of Mackinac, near the Mission of St. Ignace.

One of the first French military posts on the Great Lakes was Fort Cataraqui, established in 1673 by Frontenac at the mouth of the Cataraqui River (the present-day site of Kingston, Ontario) near the eastern end of Lake Ontario. Two years later it was granted to La Salle, who named it Fort Frontenac and used it as his base for exploring North America

The ruins of Fort Frontenac in 1783 are in the left distance, showing how the fort was situated. From a watercolor by James Peachey. (National Archives of Canada C2031)

and developing the fur trade. It was abandoned in 1689, but rebuilt of stone in more permanent form in 1694; it then was large enough to house a garrison of 700 men.

The French forts were well and strategically located. They had two main purposes: to protect against Iroquois raids on the trade routes—raids that continued or were threatened during the entire existence of New France, as French Canada was known—and to block the English colonies east of the Alleghenies from the interior lands that France claimed. A chain of forts extended along the St. Lawrence River to Lake Ontario, turned on the hinge of Fort Niagara, went to the southern shore of Lake Erie, thence southward along the Allegheny and Ohio Rivers to the Mississippi. Another chain of forts began on the Great Lakes and extended south along the Mississippi to New Orleans. Still another went westward to Lake Winnipeg and beyond to the foothills of the Rockies. Altogether there were perhaps 75 of these forts; they were of varying permanence, ranging from simple blockhouses to extensive works, and the exact number was never fixed. Among those south of Lake Erie were such familiar names as Forts Le Boeuf and Duquesne and among those in the Illinois country were forts Vincennes and Kaskaskia. On the Great Lakes the three main links in the chain were Fort Michilimackinac; Fort Ponchartrain at Detroit, where by 1757 there was also a French settlement of two hundred houses; and Fort Niagara. During the period of French control there was one British strong point on the Lakes; it was at Oswego.

On a headland on the southern shore of the Straits of Michilimackinac, in the year 1715, a French detachment under Constant Le Marchand de Lignery erected the stockaded Fort Michilimackinac, at the site of present-day Mackinaw City. (It perhaps should be noted that "Mackinac," whether standing by itself or acting as the latter part of the word "Michilimackinac," is pronounced "Mackinaw." One of the difficulties of putting Indian languages into the Latin alphabet has been finding reasonable spellings. The fur trader Peter Pond, writing in 1773, probably had the best solution when he spelled it "Mackena.")

These straits were a crossroads. Eastward lay the chain of Great Lakes and St. Lawrence River forts. Southward were Lake Michigan and the Mississippi River forts. Westward ran the forts of Lake Superior and beyond. Through the straits passed such names as Nicolet, Jolliet, Tonti, and La Salle. Through them also passed many lesser Frenchmen; as Lahontan wrote in 1688, "they cannot avoid passing this way, when they go to the seats of the *Illinese* and the *Oumamis,* or the *Bay des Puants* (Green Bay), and to the river of *Missisipi.*" From the straits, from the mission of St. Ignace on the northern shore, Father Marquette carried his religious teachings as far south as present-day Arkansas. From them, from this very fort a little later, would go war parties to fight the English and their Indian allies.

As the sound of axes felling trees and shaping logs rang across the headland, de Lignery must have been well satisfied with the location he had chosen. It was close to the water at the northernmost tip of the blunt, thrusting point of land that divides Lakes Huron and Michigan, or *Lac des Hurons* and *Lac des Illinois* to the French. It stood between the vast green forests of Michigan and the ever-changing blue and gray waters of the straits. Its six cannon were small—they had, after all, to be carried there by canoe—but they gave it added strength. It commanded the straits far better than the older fort—abandoned in 1698—that was located on the far shore beside the mission of Saint Ignace. The last commander of

Plan of Fort Michilimackinac, 1749. (National Archives of Canada (C75122)

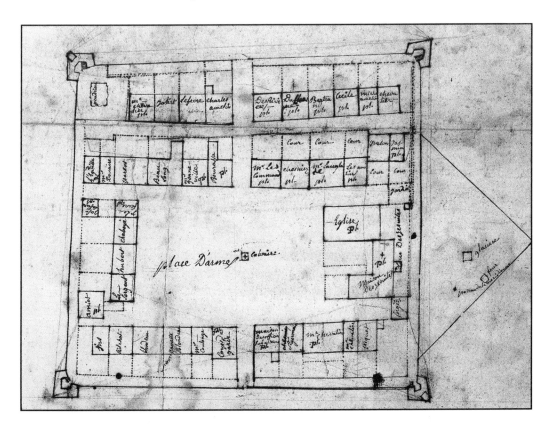

that older fort, Antoine de La Mothe Cadillac, who found time during his tour of duty to muse on the possibility that the Indians were "descended from the Hebrews and were originally Jews," was also the strongest advocate of abandoning the site. But the straits were too important to be left unfortified, and this new site, though more exposed to wind, waves, and snow, was much superior to the old one for its military purpose.

The main function of the new fort was to control and protect the fur trade. It quickly became the center of a depot and transfer point for the traders. Canoe brigades, arriving from Montreal, would pause there to take on food and make necessary repairs before going north and west to Lake Superior or south to Lake Michigan. As the fur-bearing animals were annihilated in the Great Lakes region and the trade expanded northwestward, Frenchmen from Lake Winnipeg and beyond would come as far east as Michilimackinac, where they would meet the canoe brigades from Montreal. Eastward-bound furs would be transferred to the Montreal canoes and westward-bound supplies would be transferred to the north canoes. A major reason that Cadillac had abandoned the older fort here and had established instead a major French outpost at Detroit was that the land and climate at Detroit were better suited to agriculture. Not enough food could be raised at Michilimackinac to reprovision the canoe brigades. But the importance of the place turned out to be so great that much of the corn raised at Cadillac's Detroit was sent to Mackinac to provision the fur traders who halted there.

Soon after the fort was built a mission was established there. Indians came to the post in order to trade, to visit the missionaries, and from time to time in order to confer with its commander. Inside the walls lived the families of men stationed there on official business. Outside lived those of traders, whose wives were often Indian; one of the strengths of the French in the New World was that unlike many Europeans they accepted the Indians as people.

A major figure of Michilimackinac, born there in 1729, was Charles de Langlade, descended on the side of his father, a French trader, from a noble family and on the side of his mother, sister of war chiefs, from the Ottawa nation. As a small boy he was taken by his Indian uncles on war parties; they believed that his presence brought them luck, and it always seemed to. When he grew older he led his own war parties against enemies of the Ottawas and the French. Then he became a cadet in the French army (there were no military academies; a cadet, as an apprentice officer, performed such normal duties as were assigned to him).

By the late 1740s the contest was well under way between the English and the French in the Great Lakes region. England, further advanced industrially than France, could provide better and cheaper manufactured goods. English traders, coming overland to the Ohio Valley, were undercutting French traders and drawing the allegiance of the Indians there away to the British. An expedition from Montreal in 1749 found the British traders well entrenched in Ohio and the Indians of the region unwilling to parley with the Frenchmen. In due course word of the problem reached distant Michilimackinac. Charles de Langlade and the post commander decided that something should be done. In 1752 Langlade set out for the Ohio country with 250 warriors and a few French soldiers, demolished the Miami Indian village of Pickawillany, and killed or captured the British fur traders who made their headquarters there.

In later years Langlade and some of the warriors from the Mackinac region were part of the French force that defeated General Braddock as he marched toward Fort Duquesne, and they also fought the British on Lake Champlain. In the meantime Langlade was promoted to ensign. He saw the French defeated at the Plains of Abraham in September 1759 and left Montreal just before the city surrendered in September 1760. Back at Michilimackinac he reported to the garrison commander, Captain de Beaujeau, that the worst had occurred: New France had fallen. The captain ordered his small command of slightly over a hundred soldiers into canoes and headed south to the French settlements in Illinois. Charles de Langlade remained at Michilimackinac in command of the deserted fort, in the midst of a few remaining traders and the Indians. It was late in September, 1761, that he surrendered the fort to Captain Henry Balfour and his British soldiers.

Detroit during the French regime contrasted strongly with Michilimackinac. It was a well developed town, but not much of a fort. A British captive, Charles Stuart, who was held there for a time in 1755, after his release described the fortifications in unflattering terms.

> The Fort DeTroit is a Stockade, Its a Square with Bastions and the Side next the Water had Three Bastions, But they have no Cannon in the Fort or Settlement Except a Small Mortar wch its said they have in one of their Stores—The Fort takes in abt 4 (or 5) Acres of

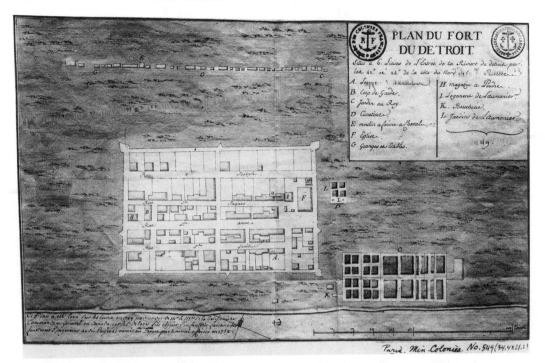

Ground and Contains abt 70 Houses wch are Built of Logs & Covered with Boards of abt an Inch Thick, Cut at a Saw Mill But have No defense agt Bombs and the Side of the Fort Next the Water is Very Weak and may be Easily Thrown Down by Mens Pushing against it, they have no Earth Thrown Up agt the Stockades nor Liners for the Seams Except some Small Stakes of abt 5 or 6 Foot high and People with Small Arms from without may Easily Kill those in it thro' the Openings between the Stockades—the Houses in the Fort are Built in Streets and are a much Better defence than the Fort itself.

Luckily for the defenders, Fort Ponchartrain as it was known never saw action.

Plan of the Fort of Detroit, 1749. Detroit was a palisaded town that Cadillac established in 1701 and named Fort Ponchartrain in honor of his French patron, Minister Ponchartrain. In 1710 Cadillac left Detroit to become governor of Louisiana. The name of Ponchartrain for the fort seems to have faded after his departure, and the place became known simply as Detroit—"The Straits." It was turned over to the British in 1760. (National Archives of France, Center for Overseas Archives, DFC Amérique septentrionale 549C, all reproduction rights reserved.)

In 1722, British fur traders from Albany set up a post at the mouth of the Oswego River where it entered Lake Ontario, midway of the southern shore. The French reacted in alarm to the news of "this establishment on territory which has been considered, from all time, to belong to France." To protect the traders from the French and Indians, Governor William Burnet of New York in 1727 began construction of a two-story "house of strength" on the west side of the river. In 1741 and 1743 this Fort Oswego was enlarged and improved.

On the outbreak of the French and Indian War in May of 1756, William Shirley, governor of the Massachusetts Bay Colony, was appointed a major general and dispatched to the mouth of the Oswego River. As part of a two-pronged thrust, he was to move against French-held Fort Niagara from that point while General Edward Braddock moved against it from Fort Duquesne, which he would surely take with his superior force. Shirley was slow in getting started, and after Braddock's defeat the attack was cancelled entirely, but meanwhile the governor had further enlarged and strengthened Fort Oswego (renaming it Fort Pepperel), had built at a short distance west of the river a small defensive position that was called Fort George (and that quickly won the nickname Fort Rascal because it was scarcely tenable), and had built an eight-pointed log structure called Fort Ontario on the height of land commanding the eastern side of the river mouth.

In June, 1756 the French under the Marquis de Montcalm attacked at Oswego—where Col. James Mercer was now in command—but were driven off. Neither adequate supplies nor reinforcements had been sent to the post, however, and a much larger French attack on August 10-14 captured all of the Oswego forts. Mercer was killed in the attack, which was followed by an event that was to become distressingly common in frontier warfare; the Indian allies of the French massacred more than a hundred British prisoners. The French destroyed all of the British forts and departed.

But in the summer of 1758 Col. John Bradstreet came up the Mohawk and down the Oswego River with "Bradstreet's Boatmen"—a force of about three thousand provincial soldiers, New England whalemen, and sailors—who struck across Lake Ontario in their whaleboats and bateaux to destroy Fort Frontenac without losing a man. The British were now on the offensive; in 1759 they established field fortifications at the Fort Ontario location and used the Oswego River mouth as their base for an attack on Fort Niagara.

On the high point of land overlooking the Niagara River where it flows into Lake Ontario, LaSalle in 1678 had constructed a log palisade. It fell into disuse, but the French rebuilt it in 1686—and abandoned it again in 1688. In 1726 they established a far more permanent post there, however, building a three-story stone structure with a steeply pitched roof—a French provincial chateau in appearance—designed by a military engineer named Gaspard de Lery. Why a military engineer to build a chateau, even one in the wilderness? Because the structure which the Indians were told was to be a storehouse—which was true enough—was also to be a fort.

It had thick stone walls, heavy oak shutters, and third-floor dormers that housed six-pounder cannon standing on a reinforced gun deck. The ground-floor windows were also heavily barred, and all shutters were pierced with loopholes through which muskets could be fired.

The fort was a trading post, but it had a more important function. It controlled the most direct route by which the French in Quebec were able to communicate with the French in Ohio, Illinois, and Louisiana. Messages, supplies, trade goods, and reinforcements came by water to the harbor in the river mouth, were taken laboriously over the portage to Lake Erie, and went on from there either southward over the Allegheny-Ohio River system or westward over the Lakes. Bales of fur being sent to Montreal travelled in the opposite direction. Neither the French posts on the Great Lakes nor those in Ohio were likely to be taken as long as Niagara stood.

By 1755 the situation between the French and British colonies was growing tense; the following year would see the French and Indian War. The British had a foothold at nearby Oswego. And so Captain Pouchot of the Regiment of Bearn, an officer who had commanded other French frontier posts, arrived at Niagara to assume command and improve the defenses. During 1755-56 he supervised construction of earthworks stretching from the lake to the river across the base of the point on which the chateau-fort stood. Stone and wooden structures supplemented the earthworks, and at one corner was a gate

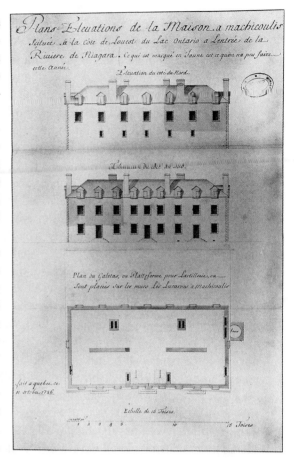

Plan of the initial stone building at Fort Niagara, constructed by the French in 1726. The shaded areas (upper right on northern side, upper left on southern side) show what remained to be completed in 1727. The plan at bottom is the top-floor gun platform. Because the building was in Iroquois territory, and the Iroquois had steadfastly opposed the building of a fort there, this was a fort disguised as a large French colonial "house" that purportedly was to be only a trading post. (National Archives of Canada C16289)

with a drawbridge. The broad, cleared plain in front gave a clear field of fire to the defenders.

In July of 1759 the British launched their attack from Oswego. General John Pridaux (pronounced "Priddy") commanded 3,000 soldiers, half of them provincials, who came along the southern shore of Lake Ontario toward Niagara in a fleet of heavily laden bateaux, whaleboats, and canoes. Pridaux also had several hundred Indians under Sir William Johnson. The swarm of boats moved close along the shore in order that the few French naval vessels on the lake would not see them. On July 6 the expedition reached a place four miles from the fort and disembarked, still undiscovered by the French. A thick forest lay between them and the cleared plain fronting the fort. At six in the evening a small hunting party of French soldiers blundered into some of the British force's Indian scouts, who seized two, but a third escaped and ran back to the fort.

Captain Pouchot sent out a reconnaissance detachment, which fell back before two hundred muskets firing volleys from behind cover. He realized then that he must be facing British Regulars, so next morning he sent messages calling

Plan of Fort Niagara, 1726. At the tip of the point the initial stone building—today called the "French Castle"—is surrounded by a palisade that makes a four-bastioned square. So far as is known, the second palisade, blocking off the point, was never built. As Iroquois villages were routinely surrounded by palisades (though without bastions), the inner line would not cause any objections. (National Archives of Canada C 16288)

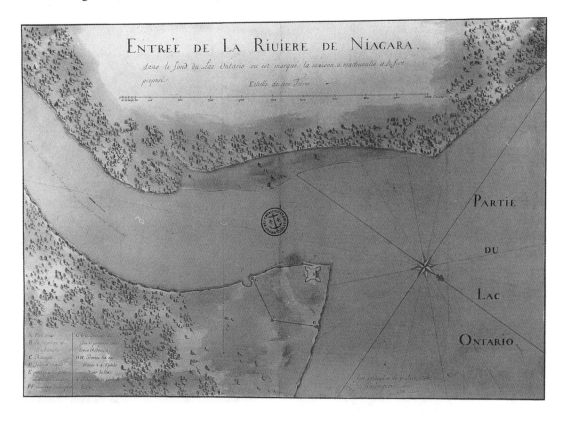

on the French commanders farther south and west for help. On the night of the 9th the British broke ground for their first trench. They also dragged whaleboats through the forest, around the fort, and launched them on the river above the fort at a place called La Belle Famille. With the boats they carried men and cannon across the river. Against the attacking force Pouchot had about 600 soldiers, plus an indefinite number of Indians.

The English approach trench zig-zagged forward, roughly parallel to the lake shore. Branching from it were other trenches, where artillery batteries were emplaced. On the 11th, eight mortars were fired from a point near the beginning of the trench system. On the 13th a mortar battery opened fire 300 yards closer to the fort. Next day a heavier battery went into action seventy yards nearer the fort.

On July 20th the afternoon sun was slowly disappearing behind the earthworks of Fort Niagara. The shadows reached toward the English trenches that extended from the forest a thousand yards away and crossed the plain to within a hundred yards of the French fort. The two sides steadily exchanged small arms and cannon fire. General Pridaux and his second in command, Col. John Johnstone of the New York Provincials, walked to the head of the trenches, discussing what was to be done that night. Suddenly Johnstone recoiled and fell dead, struck by a musket ball that entered the side of his chest. An hour later, as darkness came, General Pridaux walked through a nearby trench. One of his light mortars fired just as he stepped in front of it. The shell blew off his head.

Thus, on the night of July 20, 1759, command of the British troops before Fort Niagara passed to Sir William Johnson (no relative of Colonel Johnstone), a tall, muscu-

Sir William Johnson, who captured Fort Niagara from the French. From a miniature on ivory by an unknown artist. (National Archives of Canada C83497)

lar man of 44 with a strong jaw and one-sided smile, who held the king's commission as Colonel of the Six Nations. It was an unusual commission, but it now made him the senior officer present. Working with Indians, this Irish immigrant who had risen to baronet had few equals on the British side. In formal warfare, however, his experience was scant.

But Sir William pressed on with energy, pushing the trenches forward under cover of heavy musket and artillery fire. On the 22nd the British fire knocked three of the five artillery pieces on the lake bastion of the fort off their mounts, killing or wounding ten French artillerymen and wounding the artillery officer slightly, knocked down one wall of the bastion, and blew a number of large holes in the earth. The British poured both musket fire and shot and grape from their cannon into the breach in the wall, continuing through the night and into the next day. On the 23rd ten English whaleboats, manned by volunteers, were posted in the lake off the end of the trenches, and they too directed musket fire at the opening.

That day Sir William was thinking of assaulting the fort, when there arrived at La Belle Famille four Indian ambassadors from the tribes allied with the French in the south and west. They held a council with Johnson's Indians in his presence, presenting them with five belts as a token that they did not wish to fight their fellow Indians. They said that 600 Frenchmen and a thousand Indians were coming, and they asked Johnson's Iroquois allies to stand aside from the battle. The Iroquois agreed to do so. Johnson carefully maintained his fatherly bearing, but he knew that he now had to cope with Iroquois who suddenly thought the British might be defeated and who wanted no part of that defeat for themselves.

The four Indians then went on into the fort under a white flag and gave Pouchot letters from the French officers leading the approaching force, who asked how they could best relieve the siege. Knowing that Sir William would read his answer, Pouchot wrote referring to his letter of the 10th (in which he suggested that they come down the west side of the river) without repeating what was in it, and then gave a summary of the English dispositions. He made four copies of the letter, one for each Indian, so that if the English seized one copy the others might still get through. The four Indians ate a meal in the fort and then went out again with their flag. They passed through the English lines and once again held council with the Indians there. One of them was induced by the English to give up Pouchot's letter, but when they finally departed the other copies went with them and were delivered.

Johnson responded quickly to the new threat, moving 150 of the light infantry (picked companies from each regiment) to take position behind hastily constructed breastworks at La Belle Famille, astride the portage road leading along the east bank of the river toward Lake Erie, and to give the alarm if the French approached. He held a reserve of several companies in position to join them if necessary. On the 24th, as the French approached, Sir William moved the additional men into position.

Soon afterward the main French army arrived, coming directly down the portage road and making a frontal attack on the British position, instead of following the course Pouchot had recommended. At this time there was a heavy rain shower and the French seemed to have trouble in firing their wet weapons. The English volleys also had their effect. Then the English leaped out from behind their breastworks and closed with their opponents.

The French gave way in front and attempted to move around the English left flank. The English shifted part of their men to meet them, and the Mohawks—the tribe on which the English could most depend—attacked from the forest on the French flank. Most of the Frenchmen broke and ran; the small number who stood and fought were either killed or captured. As soon as the French began to retreat, all of the other Iroquois who had been wavering on the sidelines were off in hot pursuit with tomahawks and knives, whooping and screaming their battle cries as they butchered the stragglers.

The British and the freshly inspired Iroquois pursued the fleeing men through the woods for five miles. Less than an hour after it had started, the battle was over. Among the captured French officers were Captain Aubrey, the French commander, and Captain de Lignery, the second in command. Why these expert bush fighters came down the east side of the river and made a frontal attack against prepared positions was never explained. Possibly they misunderstood Pouchot's message. Even so, their approach was surprisingly careless; overconfidence seems the only answer.

About four o'clock, after vigorous firing had resumed on both sides, the English drums beat a signal to cease fire in the trenches and an English officer appeared on the plain with a white flag. He was brought into the fort and delivered a message from Johnson telling of the French defeat and giving the names of the French officers who had been captured. Pouchot, suspecting a trick, sent a captain to see whether the officers were actually captives. The French captain was admitted to the English camp, where he saw the wounded de Lignery (who later died of his wounds) and a number of others in a little woods near Sir William's tent. He was so overcome with emotion that he hardly could speak to them, and he returned to tell Pouchot what he had observed.

The fort was terribly battered. Everyone in it was exhausted. At best they could hold out only a few more days, and there no longer was any hope of relief. Pouchot called in the English officer and told him that he would capitulate if the garrison could march out with the honors of war and be returned to Montreal. This message was carried to Johnson, who replied that he could send them only to some place on the English side where they might be exchanged. Throughout the night messages passed back and forth between the two commanders, working out the conditions of surrender.

Plan of Fort Niagara in 1759, after it had been developed into a true fort. The trenches and batteries of the attacking British force are to the right of the fort. (National Archives of Canada, C29884)

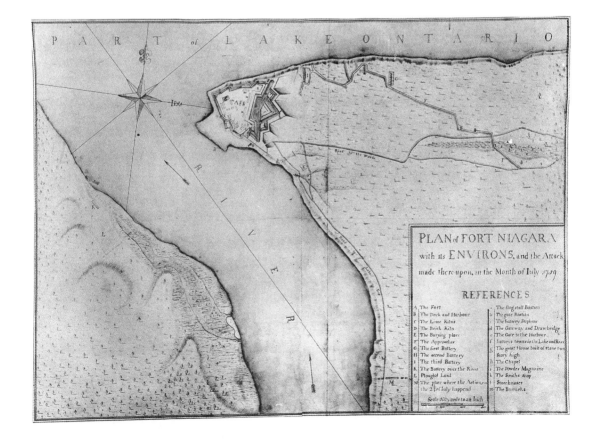

Both Pouchot and Johnson had foremost in mind the massacre at Fort William Henry, on Lake George, two years before. There the French had taken an English fort, had disarmed their English captives, and then had lost control of their own Indians. The Indians fell on the unarmed men and slaughtered them. The situation now was reversed. Outside the walls Johnson had a horde of aroused Indians. The French garrison was surrendering. Both commanders now hoped above all else to prevent another massacre. The first article of capitulation they agreed on was that the garrison would march out with arms and baggage, drums beating, and with a small cannon.

Early on the morning of July 25 Pouchot drew up the garrison in line of battle on the parade ground, their arms in their hands and haversacks at their feet. At seven o'clock the drawbridge creaked and rattled down. Four companies of British grenadiers marched to the gates and took possession of them. They were followed by the 44th Regiment (which had been at Braddock's defeat), which marched through the main gates onto the parade ground, with drums beating and colors flying, and formed in line across from the garrison. Captain Pouchot and Colonel Sir William Johnson took their posts in front of their troops. They exchanged salutes. Pouchot surrendered formally. Johnson accepted his sword and then graciously returned it. Fort Niagara was officially British.

Sir William had posted soldiers at every possible entrance to the fort, to keep the Indians out of it. Within an hour, however, Indians had climbed the walls on all sides and there were over five hundred of them in the fort. Some at first tried to take the weapons from some of the French soldiers; one English officer was slashed by an Indian knife when he tried to disperse them. The French firmly refused to give up their weapons.

A strong northwest wind had come up, which made it impossible to launch the boats. The French garrison stood there surrounded by Indians over whom the British had only nominal control. Tension grew. The Indians proceeded to loot the fort, taking even the ironwork and the hinges off the doors, breaking open and spilling barrels of flour, and taking five or six hundred bales of fur from the storerooms. For thirty hours the garrison waited on the parade ground while unruly Indians prowled around them, looting or smashing everything in the fort.

In the afternoon of the 26th the wind abated. Finally the French marched out of the fort toward the beach, muskets on their shoulders, drums beating, and two large artillery pieces at the head of the column, with cannoneers carrying lighted matches. The British escort watched the Indians as much as it did the prisoners. As the soldiers reached the English boats the Frenchmen laid down their arms and at once embarked and pulled out into the lake, even though the waves still were high. They turned then toward Oswego; from there they would be sent to New York.

In seizing Fort Niagara, Johnson smashed the hinge on which the French chain of forts depended and established the British on the Great Lakes. He cut Ohio, Detroit, and Illinois from Canada, thus chopping in two the French holdings in North America. He also destroyed the last French army in the west, which was gathering to descend on Pittsburgh when Pouchot's call for help diverted it to Niagara. Montreal itself was now outflanked and the fall of New France was only a matter of time. No wonder that the toast of the day in New York was "Johnson forever!"

2
THE BRITISH ON THE
GREAT LAKES

After the French surrender of Canada, Major Robert Rogers came over Lake Erie to take command at Detroit. Part way there, near the site of present-day Cleveland, he was intercepted by the Indian leader Pontiac who wanted to know his business in the Indian country and who then escorted him to Detroit. This old print shows a romanticised version of the event, which was a forerunner of Pontiac's war against the British. (Library of Congress)

Following the surrender of New France, the British took over the major posts on the Great Lakes. The flamboyant Major Robert Rogers accepted Detroit from its French commander on November 29, 1760. (There was a shadow of things to come when the Ottawa chief, Pontiac, intercepted Rogers en route to Detroit, demanded to know the Englishman's business in the Indian country, and then escorted him to the post.) During the following winter British detachments occupied many of the other forts, and the next year they completed the occupation of the more distant ones such as Michilimackinac and La Baye (which had been erected by the French on Green Bay in 1717).

Most of the British, unlike the French, had small talent in dealing with Indians. General Jeffrey Amherst, who had led the British forces to victory in North America with some skill, adopted a disastrous Indian policy. He viewed the Indians with contempt; a few scattered soldiers could surely keep such barbarians subdued. He refused to continue the former diplomatic presentation of gifts to the tribes. In vain such British experts on Indian life as Sir William Johnson protested; Amherst was firm.

The first English settlers began to encroach on Indian land west of the Alleghenies. British traders, who now had no competition in their dealings with the Indians, were often more rapacious than the French had been. At the same time the French woodsmen and merchants who remained throughout the region assured the Indians that if only they would rise against the British, the French government would return to help them. Throughout 1761 and 1762 Pontiac worked to create a confederacy of the tribes throughout the Great Lakes region. In spring of 1763 he struck, to the complete surprise of the British. The Indians took all of the posts in the west except Detroit, Fort Niagara, and Fort Pitt (formerly the French Fort Duquesne).

At Michilimackinac on June 2, 1763 a group of local Chippewas played a game of lacrosse with some visiting Sauk outside the walls of the fort. The post commander, Captain Etherington, had been warned that the Indians were rebellious, but he ignored the warnings. The lacrosse game built up to a crescendo of excitement in which the ball was tossed over the stockade and the players rushed after it through the gate. Inside were stationed Indian women who carried axes and sawed-off muskets under their blankets; they handed the weapons to the braves who proceeded to slaughter the unsuspecting British soldiers throughout the fort.

The French villagers outside the walls observed the massacre from the sidelines; it was directed not against them but against the British. Alexander Henry, one of the first British fur traders to reach the interior after the conquest of Canada, was sitting in his room in the village, writing letters. Hearing the noise he looked out, and seeing what was happening he snatched his loaded fowling piece and waited for the sound of drums signaling the soldiers to form and counterattack. But there were no drums; the surprise was complete.

Henry vaulted the fence between his house and that of the Langlade family, next door. An Indian servant woman led him up to a garret, from where he could see into the fort and watch the massacre proceeding. Then the Indians came to the Langlade house and asked if Henry was there; the family, not knowing of his presence, told the Indians that he was not and that they could look for themselves— which they proceeded to do, stumbling around in the dark garret while Henry hid as best he could.

Alexander Henry, British fur trader captured at Michilimackinac by the Indians at the outbreak of Pontiac's War, but rescued by the Chippewa chief Wawatam. (National Archives of Canada, C103612)

That night he escaped detection, but eventually he was discovered; he and the remaining British prisoners were taken away by different bands of Indians. Some were killed. He was rescued by an Indian named Wawatam, a man who had become his friend in past years and with whom he had gone through the Indian ritual making them brothers. (Henry survived, in time becoming a major figure in the fur trade and finally dying quietly in Montreal in 1824.)

During 1763 and 1764 Col. Henry Bouquet and Col. John Bradstreet waged campaigns against the Indians. By this time the tribes in the Great Lakes region were entirely dependent on the white man not only for such essentials as guns and gunpowder, but even for such small items as needles. Now the British were the only source of such things, and the British would provide nothing as long as the war continued. Also in 1763 one of the recurring smallpox plagues spread through the Indian settlements. Economics, disease, and military action, coupled with the psychological effects of France's refusal to help in any way, brought the war to an end in a series of councils and treaties during 1764 and 1765. In July 1766 Pontiac made his final settlement with Sir William Johnson under the guns of Fort Oswego.

The posts of the western Great Lakes region were gradually reoccupied by the British. Michilimackinac was regarrisoned in September 1764. It was the only point northwest of Detroit to be held by British military forces in the following years. Once they were well established, the British carried out various improvements, including the construction of new forts at Detroit, Mackinac, and Oswego.

For a time there was a mad scramble in the fur trade between Albany, Philadelphia, and those British traders who had moved to Montreal, taken on French partners, and taken over the whole French apparatus of voyageurs, canoes, and business methods. Generally, each group demanded regulations that favored it and hindered the others.

In August, 1766 Major Robert Rogers assumed command at Michilimackinac. With him came Captain James Tute who had commanded one of his ranger companies and Jonathen Carver, another former ranger officer who was also a self-taught mapmaker with an itch for exploration. Rogers's career had already ranged from national hero through fashionable author to inmate in a New York debtors' prison (his soldiers assaulted the jail and set him free). He was loaded with debt and he hoped to use his new post to advance his fortune. His burning intent now was to use Mackinac as the base from which to discover the Northwest Passage—the fabled water route through North America to the Pacific.

Tute and Carver he sent to reach the Pacific, find the western entrance to the Passage, and follow it back to Hudson Bay, its supposed eastern beginning, where generations of explorers had somehow been unable to locate it. Carver went farther than Tute, penetrating Minnesota and wintering with the Sioux, but neither man reached the Pacific. Rogers was unable to forward supplies to them and the explorers had to return again to Mackinac. Carver later published a book about his travels in which he reported quite accurately on the country he had traversed, but much less accurately on the remaining geography of North America.

When Rogers took command of the post he stepped into the middle of an argument between the Montreal fur traders, who insisted that they should have freedom to go and winter with the Indians as the French had done before them, and Sir William Johnson, now the Indian Superintendent, who upon the return of traders after Pontiac's War had ruled that they could trade with the Indians only at the established government posts, such as Mackinac, where they operated under the supervision of the commander and thus were less apt to cheat the Indians or fight with each other. This rule was better adapted to trade in the southern areas, where the Indians lived nearer the posts and where there was game for the

LE MAJOR ROBERT ROGER
Commandant en Chef les Troupes Indiennes au service des Americains

A Paris chez Esnauts et Rapilly, rue S.t Jacques a la Ville de Coutances A.P.D.R.

Above: Major Rogers, as seen in a French print (and with a French spelling of his name). "Americans" as a nationality did not exist in Rogers's day; the French term referred to British nationals living or serving in North America. (National Archives of Canada, C6875)

Next PageTop: The commanding officer's house, Fort Michilimackinac, has been restored to look much as it did when Robert Rogers lived there. (Mackinac State Historic Parks)

Next Page Bottom : Modern sketch showing Michilimackinac as it was c. 1770, shortly after Rogers commanded the fort. (Mackinac State Historic Parks)

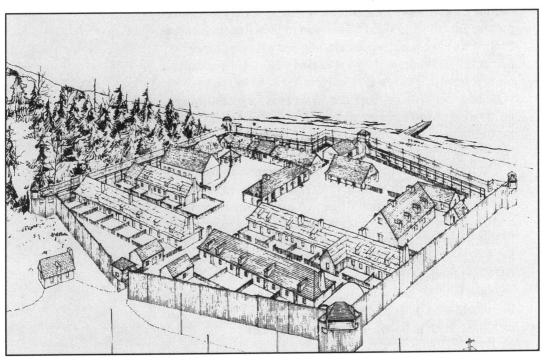

traders to subsist on, and less adapted to the northern posts—such as Mackinac—where the Indians had to go far from the posts in order to live through the winter and where the traders often could not remain in winter at all. It thus favored the Albany traders. It also counteracted the advantages of the Montreal traders who had the waterways and canoes by which they could go out to the Indians, while the traders farther south did not. Whether Johnson, a New Yorker, intentionally set out to favor the men from his own colony is a moot question.

Rogers sided with the Mackinac traders, though Johnson was his superior in Indian matters as General Sir Thomas Gage, stationed in New York, was his superior in military matters. Rogers set out to expand his territory as far as possible, travelling through the nearby country and summoning tribesmen from far and wide to councils at the post. To further these activities he gave presents to the Indians at an increasing rate, paying for them with drafts on the Indian Department.

Throughout the winter he worked on a proposal that he sent eastward next spring in the form of a petition to the Board of Trade in London. It was a direct challenge to Johnson. Let Michilimackinac, Rogers asked, be a headquarters from which trade would be carried on with Indians throughout the far reaches of the Northwest; and let it be a separate province, outside the control of the eastern colonial government and reporting directly to London. This plan to give Rogers half the continent as his own domain certainly had a flavor of megalomania, but it also showed a good deal of vision. He marshalled his arguments. The reaction in New York, however, may be imagined. Sir William labeled it "a scheme for establishing a needy man of bad circumstances and worse principles in the first authority." The proposal was duly forwarded to London, but with comments from Johnson that killed it decisively.

The tragedy moved on. Rogers had a violent argument with his secretary, a man named Potter, who then returned to Montreal and there accused Rogers of plotting treason. General Gage now had an excuse to remove a troublemaker; on his orders Rogers was arrested in November, 1767, and confined in irons at his own post during the winter. In the spring he was taken to Montreal for trial—and acquitted. But he was never returned to office and was left a ruined man whose remaining life would lead through debtors' prisons and alcoholic bouts to a quiet death in impoverished circumstances.

In the meanwhile the British Parliament, sobered by Pontiac's War and moved to further action by numerous complaints of inequities from the American frontier, set out to stop white land speculation in the western region, to control the squatters and criminals who were attracted there, and to conciliate the French inhabitants who were chafing at the lack of civil law and at some of the more repressive British regulations. Parliament passed the Quebec Act, extending French civil law as far as the Illinois country, giving control of trade in the Northwest to the Quebec fur traders, guaranteeing French inhabitants free exercise of their religion, and blocking settlement west of the Alleghenies by English colonists. With this one piece of legislation they almost assured the American Revolution. Traders, Protestant divines, Colonial land speculators, would-be settlers, and politicians all denounced the act. One of Alexander Hamilton's first political speeches attacked it. The English colonists had helped the mother country defeat the French, largely because they wanted interior North America. Now they intended to have it.

The American Revolution at first had little effect in the Great Lakes region. The British retained most of the forts there throughout it. An American drive toward Fort Niagara by Major General John Sullivan, after victory over British and Indians in upstate New York, was more intent on laying waste the countryside—in the manner of Sherman's later march through Georgia—than in capturing the fort. By the time he turned south in September he had destroyed orchards, vegetable gardens, and cornfields, and had burned more than forty Seneca and Cayuga Indian villages, sending their inhabitants scurrying to a winter of semi-starvation at Niagara.

During the Revolution the British for a time used Fort Ontario at Oswego as a base from which to launch raids into New York. Then they abandoned the fort and in 1778 American soldiers burned the buildings in it but left the walls standing. The British reoccupied it in 1782. General Washington then ordered Colonel Marinus Willett to capture the fort. Willett and about five hundred men marched through the deep snows and sub-zero temperatures of February, 1783, reached a place three-quarters of a mile from the walls—and were discovered by a party of British soldiers out cutting firewood. Three of the soldiers got back to the fort to give the alarm. Washington had specifically ordered Willett not to attack unless he could surprise the garrison, so the Americans turned

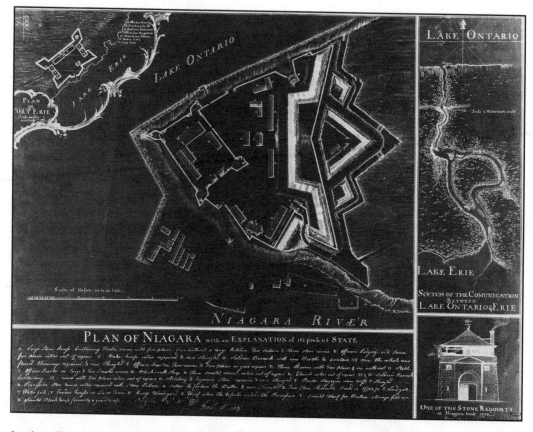

PLAN OF NIAGARA with an EXPLANATION of its present STATE

British plan of Fort Niagara as it was in 1773. Drawing of redoubt at lower right shows the original form of these structures. Plan of Fort Erie inset upper left corner shows that fort as proposed, not as it actually was. (By permission of the British Library, Kings Maps CXXI 78[1] 1773)

back to Fort Stanwix (site of modern Rome, N.Y.). There they learned that peace had been declared.

Farther west George Rogers Clark, an experienced Indian fighter and major in the militia of what was then Kentucky County of Virginia, led an expedition authorized by Governor Patrick Henry of Virginia against British-held Kaskaskia, on the Mississippi in what today is lower Illinois. Clark and nearly two hundred Virginia soldiers shot the Falls of the Ohio during a total eclipse of the sun, hid their boats some miles downstream, and proceeded on foot, arriving at the British post on July 4, 1778. They took the place by complete surprise, capturing the town and fort without a fight. Clark also occupied other nearby villages and sent a small detachment to Vincennes, where the Americans were welcomed by the French inhabitants.

At Detroit the British commander, Col. Henry Hamilton, immediately started to organize an expedition against Clark. (Hamilton was known to the Americans as the "Hair-Buyer

General" because they firmly believed that he offered bounties for colonial scalps, though most American historians of later generations have concluded that the story was false.) With nearly two hundred whites and sixty Indians he set out on October 7. Winter came as they continued their march, but despite their hardships they gathered more warriors as they went on. By December 17, when Hamilton reached Vincennes, he had five hundred men. He took the place easily. But he was weary, his supplies were low, and the rivers were flooding. He decided to wait until spring before moving against Kaskaskia, and so he released his Indians and militia to go back to the Great Lakes.

Late in January, Clark learned that the British leader had few soldiers at Vincennes but expected to gather a large force again in the spring. It was now or never for Clark. With about a hundred and thirty men, half of them local French volunteers, he set out on the seventeen-day march to Vincennes, wading through the flooded, ice-crusted countryside. The townspeople there received him as a friend and his men attacked the fort without warning to its defenders. After an all-night battle, Hamilton surrendered. Two days later he and twenty-six other British prisoners were on their way to Virginia under guard.

When Hamilton had left Detroit, command there passed to Captain Richard Lernoult. He of course knew of Clark's expedition, and soon after Hamilton's departure he also learned that an American force sent out from Fort Pitt had established itself at Lower Sandusky (present-day Fremont, Ohio) about 90 miles away from Detroit. The fort at Detroit was still much the same as it had been during the French era, weak and poorly located. Lernoult determined to build a new fort on a height of land a short distance away. He set busily to work.

Clark, learning of the activity after Hamilton's capture, sent off the cocky message to Lernoult, "I learn by your letter to Governor Hamilton that you were very busy making new works. I am glad to hear it, as it saves the Americans some expense in building." Despite the jibe, however, the news may well have deterred Clark from a move against Detroit. The fort, a stockade in the shape of an irregular four-pointed star, surrounded several acres and contained a number of buildings. It was completed in April 1779 and named Fort Lernoult, after its builder.

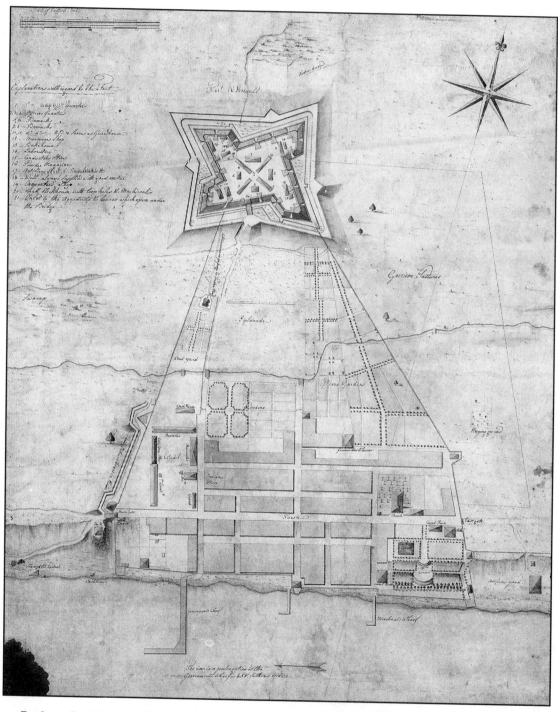

Fort Lernoult and the town of Detroit, 1779. This was a British fort, established in 1778, and named for Capt. Richard B. Lernoult, the officer who was then in command. Note the palisade that extends from the fort proper to the river, and then along the river front, in effect fortifying the entire town. After Detroit was turned over to the Americans in the person of Anthony Wayne in 1796, the fort was renamed Fort Shelby. General Hull gained unhappy fame by surrendering it to the British in 1812. After that war, during which it was retaken by the Americans, it was gradually allowed to deteriorate, was turned over to Detroit, and was torn down in 1826. (William L. Clements Library)

That autumn at Michilimackinac, Patrick Sinclair arrived to take charge. Sinclair had been an officer in the Black Watch and later, in the 1760s, had commanded ships of the Provincial Marine on the Great Lakes. Now, however, his title was Lieutenant Governor, and Mackinac was the headquarters of a great western district.

Sinclair was quite aware of the adventures of George Rogers Clark in the Illinois country and he felt that a similar thrust could well be directed at Mackinac. As he looked around the fort, weatherbeaten and poorly maintained as it was, he realized that while it commanded the straits, it could readily be approached without warning through the sand dunes behind it. He spent three days "from sun to sun" going over the island of Michilimackinac in the straits nearby. Then he sent off a letter to Quebec proposing that the fort be moved to the high bluff on the island.,

Governor Haldimand in Quebec approved, directing that the new post be named Fort Mackinac (the first time the shortened name was used officially). His approval arrived the following spring, and Sinclair set to work (as a matter of fact, he had had his men working all winter in anticipation of the approval). He bought the island from the Chippewas for £5,000, and began construction. By the summer of 1781, however, his drafts on Quebec totaled over £60,000, and Haldimand sent out three inspectors to audit his accounts. They discovered careless bookkeeping, some of it perhaps to Sinclair's personal gain. The first lieutenant governor at Mackinac resigned in September, 1782, leaving others to complete the island stronghold he had founded.

Because the war came no closer to the upper Lakes than Vincennes and Kaskaskia, fur traders on the Lakes were able to continue their efforts without interruption. Combinations of traders began to form, who pooled their stock and sent out only a few of their numbers father into the country west of Lake Superior. By 1776 one combination known as the North West Company had begun to predominate. Its members were strong individuals—the trade demanded initiative above all else—who squabbled, broke apart, and regrouped, but the company grew.

In 1778 it began to build a large fort at Grand Portage, the place on the northwestern shore of Lake Superior where cargoes left the Great Lakes and were carried nine miles to Partridge River on the first leg of the journey westward to Lake of the Woods and Lake Winnipeg. There had formerly been a small French post there, and since about 1768 British traders had had several buildings at the place, but nothing had been constructed as impressive as this; when the fort was completed in 1784 it consisted of sixteen buildings inside a substantial palisade.

It was not a military post, although the government, at the request of the traders, stationed an officer and six soldiers there for two months in the summer of 1778, "during the time which the Merchants take to transact their business at that place, for the purpose of observing order and regularity among the people who resort there." By the next summer, however, George Rogers Clark's raid had changed military priorities in the region, and the soldiers could not be spared. No similar detachment ever went again to Grand Portage. The fort, however, was well defended against Indians—and against other fur traders, for rivalry was intense. It now became the transfer point

A modern picture shows Grand Portage, the fur-trade post at the western end of Lake Superior, at its height of activity c.1780. (Grand Portage National Monument)

for the westward trade of the North West Company, where canoes from Montreal met those from the interior.

During the time that the traders from the interior met those from Montreal there were constant business meetings of the North West Company partners and a purposeful bustle among the lesser employees who were packing furs, marking fur bales, and getting ready supplies for the interior. There also was time for amusement. Daniel Harmon, who was there in 1800 wrote:

In the day time, the Natives were permitted to dance in the fort, and the Company made them a present of thirty six gallons of Shrub. In the evening, the gentlemen of the place dressed, and we had a famous ball, in the dining room. For musick, we had the bag-pipe, the violin and the flute, which added much to the interest of the occasion. At the ball, there were a number of the ladies of this country; and I was surprised to find that they could conduct with so much propriety, and dance so well.

EVOLUTION OF A FORT
FORT MACKINAC

1813

One of the earliest pictures of the island fort, seen on the bluffs in the background. The houses along the shore belong to fur traders. (McCord Museum, McGill University, Montreal M 3954)

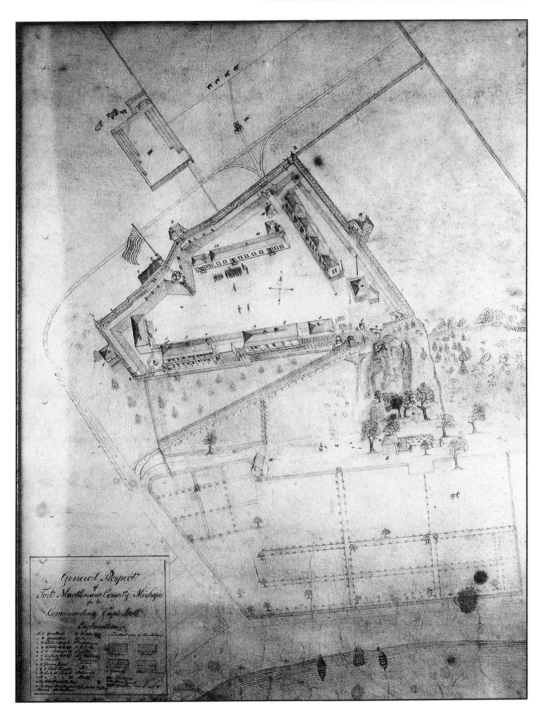

1842

This bird's-eye view of the fort was drawn by Pvt. W. Brenschutz of the U.S.
Fifth Infantry. (William L. Clements Library)

1870

Above: An 1870 drawing of Fort Mackinac, as seen from Lake Huron. (U.S. National Archives RG 77 Misc Forts, Fort Mackinac #1)

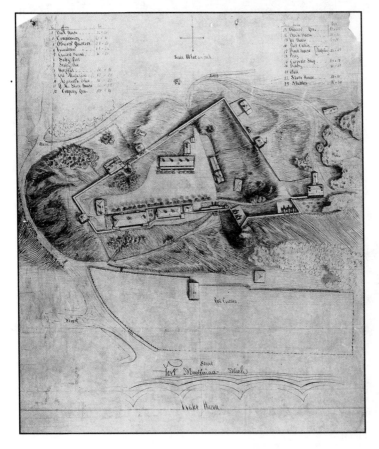

Left: Fort Mackinac is shown from a different perspective in another bird's eye view. The outline of the fort is much the same as in the 1842 view, but note how many details have changed. (U.S. National Archives RG 77, Misc Forts, Fort Mackinac #16)

1871

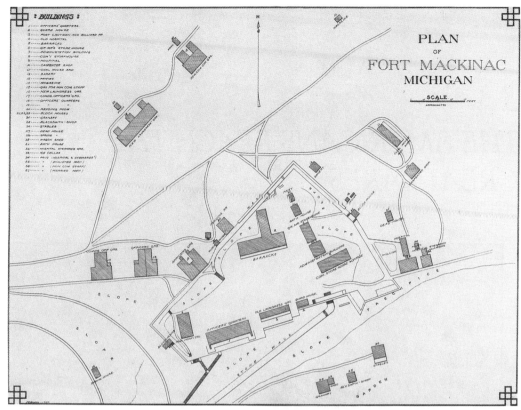

1890 ....

As with other forts at this time, some of its activities have spilled over into buildings outside the walls. (U.S. National Archives RG 92, Blueprint File, Fort Mackinac #1)

The park at the foot of the hill was once the vegetable garden for the fort. A statue of the pioneer missionary, Father Marquette, stands in the park. (Mackinac State Historic Parks)

... AND NOW

3

THE AMERICANS REACH THE GREAT LAKES

As the Revolutionary War ended, American settlers came streaming over the Alleghenies and down into the Ohio Valley. The new central government of the United States, needing time to resolve the conflicting claims of several states to the region, forbad the settlers to move in until it could make up its mind. They ignored it. In 1787 Congress passed the Northwest Ordnance, establishing the Northwest Territory in the Ohio country, and the stream of settlers became a river.

The Treaty of Paris, which in 1783 officially ended the war, gave the land south of the Great Lakes to the United States. The Indians of course were not consulted. And the British, expecting that the arguing, ineffectual government of the United States would fall apart in short order, retained their forts along the southern shores of the Lakes in what nominally was American territory. Thus the inexorable flow of settlers came into a region held by Indians who had no desire to give up their land and who were backed by the commanders of the British forts, who provided them weapons and guidance. Many of the settlers for their part believed that the only good Indian was a dead Indian, and there were constant massacres and retaliations on both sides.

Hoping to stem the slaughter, Congress in the fall of 1790 dispatched a Revolutionary War veteran, Josiah Harmar, with a motley army of some fifteen hundred men, on a punitive expedition against the Indians. Only about three hundred of Harmar's men were "Continentals"—regulars—and the rest Pennsylvania and Kentucky militia with varying degrees of experience and discipline. The Indians withdrew ahead of the force, about half the militia deserted en route, and when the army finally found some Indians it disobeyed Harmar's orders and was defeated.

Detroit waterfront in 1794, shortly before the United States took over the city. Note the palisade that surrounded, and in effect, fortified, the entire town. (Burton Historical Collection, Detroit Public Library)

The following autumn Arthur St. Clair, elderly governor of the Northwest Territory, took to the field with an equally poor army of about twenty-five hundred. His expected supplies did not follow him, he suffered desertions, and he sent his best Continentals back to look for the supply train and the deserters. After camping on the night of November 3 on the bank of the Wabash River, in the middle of the forest without any fortifications, the army was attacked next morning with utter surprise by a large force of Indians. It was completely routed. Six hundred and thirty of its members were killed and nearly three hundred were wounded.

Horrified by the disaster, President Washington and Congress began to put together a real army. They called out of retirement the Revolutionary War hero Anthony Wayne. Congress in 1792 formed the first true United States Army, The Legion of the United States, and Wayne was put in command of it. Mad Anthony never had the nearly five thousand men and officers that he was theoretically authorized, and he had constant problems with supplies, pay, disease, and graft, but he formed and trained an army, first near Pittsburgh and later at a camp near Cincinnati at a place that he wryly named Hobson's Choice. In October, 1793 he marched north to a point that was roughly half way between the Ohio River and Lake Erie and near the present-day Ohio-Indiana boundary; there he erected Fort Greene Ville (named for Wayne's old Revolutionary War comrade Nathanael Greene, the name later shortened to that of present-day

General Anthony Wayne, the Revolutionary War hero, was recalled to active duty to train and command the U.S. armies in the Old Northwest. He defeated the Indians, who were backed by the British, at the Battle of Fallen Timbers. (Ohio Historical Society)

Greenville in Ohio), a stockaded fort about six hundred yards long and three hundred wide, with integral blockhouses at key points and nine more outlying blockhouses, each about a hundred and fifty yards from the main wall. Inside the stockade were buildings to quarter the army, administrative and supply buildings, and a "laboratory" for making ammunition.

With Fort Greene Ville largely completed, Wayne set his engineer, Major Henry Burbeck, to building a smaller fort twenty miles farther north—on the exact site of St. Clair's defeat. He located it with full awareness of the psychological effect of the place on both his own men and the Indians. In order to camp there, the soldiers had to remove the bones just below the surface to make level places for their tents; as they built the structure they recovered over six hundred skulls. It was a rectangular, stockaded structure with a blockhouse twenty feet square at each corner. Each blockhouse was placed at an angle to the stockade, so that three of its sides faced outward. Some of the cannon in the blockhouses were recovered from the old battlefield, where the Indians had hidden them, and immediately on completion of the post in late December, 1793, Wayne honored those killed in the defeat with "three times three discharges from the artillery that was lost on that fatal day." He named the post Fort Recovery. It was garrisoned with three hundred men. The fort became a base for reconnaissance parties that scouted out a northward route for his army; and once the army took the field again, Fort Recovery would help guard his supply line.

In spring 1794 the British established a new post called Fort Miamis on the Maumee River near Lake Erie and gathered around it war parties summoned from Indian tribes throughout the Great Lakes region to oppose Wayne's advance. By mid-June, nearly two thousand braves had assembled. On June 30 they descended on Fort Recovery, the location of which they considered a particular affront. A supply column had reached the fort the night before and its horses were grazing outside the walls. On the morning of the 30th the Indians attacked, drove off three hundred pack horses, and killed or captured some of the soldiers who were outside the walls. The escort of the pack train, a detachment of cavalry, dashed out from the fort under heavy fire, lost about half its strength in the ensuing fight, and retreated while the garrison sent out an infantry force to support it. For a time soldiers, Indians, and horses were mixed in a wild fight, but the soldiers were soon driven back inside the fort by the vastly superior number of attackers. The excited Indians circled about Fort Recovery all day, firing; at midnight when the fort commander, Captain Alexander Gibson, sat down to write his account of the day he noted "they are still round the Garrison giving and receiving shots and yells." Unable to reduce the fort, however, the Indians withdrew by the next morning and, to the disgust of some of the British officers with them, a number began to drift away in disappointment.

It was almost a month later, at eight in the morning of July 28, a hot, humid Ohio summer day, that Wayne's army left Greene Ville and began the march northward toward Lake Erie and battle. He had about two thousand of his own men and had been reinforced by fifteen hundred mounted Kentucky volunteers under General Charles Scott. That day, and each day of the march that followed, Wayne tried to halt in midafternoon so that his men had time to build field fortifications around their encampment; he had no intention of letting them suffer the fate of St. Clair's army.

The general stopped about twenty miles north of Fort Recovery to build Fort Adams, a two-blockhouse stockaded position, smaller than Recovery but similar to it. In the partly finished post he left forty of his sick and injured men in the charge of a Lieutenant Underhill. The lieutenant was acutely unhappy at being left in such a position, but Wayne felt that he had to move forward with all of his effective force as quickly as possible. (As it developed, Underhill's fears were not well grounded; Fort Adams was never attacked.)

By August 8 Wayne was in the middle of the Indian country, at the place where the Auglaize River flows into the Maumee. All about him were wide fields of Indian corn. At the juncture of the rivers was a large, abandoned Indian village. The soldiers, hungry for vegetables, helped themselves from the fields and gardens. Wayne issued a general order, congratulating "the federal army upon taking possession of the grand emporium of the hostile Indians of the West," and in celebration ordered the quartermaster to issue one gill of whiskey to each man. Then they began work on yet another post, Fort Defiance. Built in the pattern of Fort Recovery, it was even stronger, with a deep ditch outside the stockade and a covered way from the fort to the place where the two rivers joined, through which water and supplies could be taken into the fort.

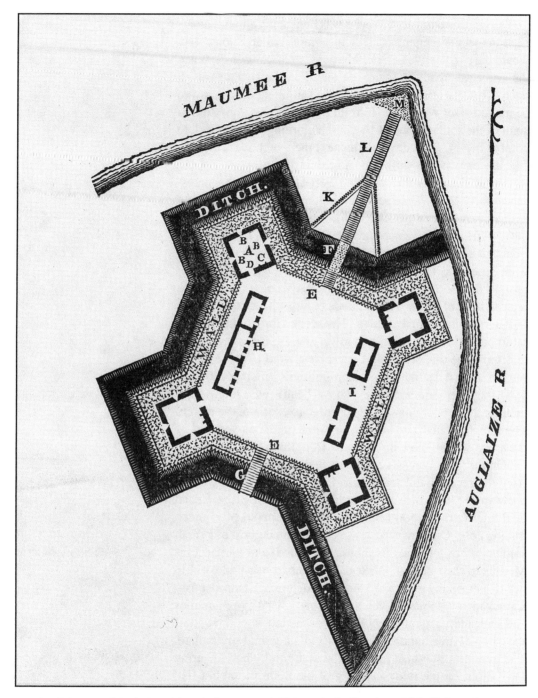

Fort Defiance, built by Anthony Wayne in the summer of 1794, was the final base he established before going on to fight the Indians and British at the Battle of Fallen Timbers. Today the location is the town of Defiance, Ohio. (Ohio Historical Society)

During this campaign Wayne was constantly ill with an affliction that contemporary medicine simply called "Gout." (He would die two years later from "the gout in his stomach.") When the army was ready to march on the 15th, the general was in agony from an attack and the surgeon said that he was unfit to be moved. But Wayne had himself lifted onto his horse, out of sight of the soldiers, and at five in the morning the approach to combat began. That day and the next the march was cut short because of Wayne's suffering and exhaustion.

While the army was building Fort Defiance, a reconnaissance party that Wayne sent out captured an Indian man and woman and learned from them that the tribesmen intended to make a firm stand against Wayne's force. Seven hundred warriors had assembled for that purpose and another four hundred were expected. The British Indian Agent in the region had also promised a thousand white soldiers. Wayne sent the male Indian and one of his own scouts under a flag of truce to ask if the Indians wanted to make peace. His scout, Christopher Miller, returned at this time with the answer; the Indians would have to discuss the matter among themselves; would Wayne please remain at Fort Defiance and stop building forts for ten days until they decided. Wayne, whose health was improving, thought this a poor answer. He decided to continue the march. The Indian scouts, who kept close watch on the movements of the army, would know his decision from that action.

On the 18th Wayne's army reached a point only six miles from the recently erected British Fort Miamis. They were at the Maumee Rapids, at a famous Indian gathering place, Roche de Bout, where there still could be seen the remains of a French trading post. Unknown to the Americans, an outpost of British soldiers there fell back as they approached, and alerted Fort Miamis to their arrival. Next day Wayne, much improved in health, personally supervised the construction of Camp Deposit, a stockaded area inside which the army left its extra supplies and baggage. Captain Zebulon Pike was left in command of the camp, with a hundred Regulars and a hundred militiamen. The quartermaster also remained at that point when the army moved out on the rainy morning of the 20th, through a flat, wooded, swampy countryside.

They had covered four miles and the weather had cleared by eleven that morning. Then on high ground ahead there appeared a body of mounted Indians. The detachment of militia cavalrymen who were riding as a reconnaissance force ahead of the army dropped back in panic. Bugle calls and drum signals sounded as the soldiers moved to combat. The right wing of federal troops, nearest the sudden collapse of the militia cavalry screen, quickly formed for battle; the frightened militiamen galloped right through the regulars, hacking away at those who tried to stop them.

The mounted Indians, two deep, in a line almost two miles long and running at an angle to the river that lay on Wayne's right, were attempting to turn his left flank and force the army into the river. Wayne, however, sent the main body of Scott's militia cavalry to outflank the Indians in turn; when the Indians saw what was happening they fell back. They retreated across an open prairie to a place where a wind storm had twisted and uprooted the trees of a forest. As a second tactic, they planned to draw the Americans to this point and make a stand in the fallen timbers. But only a third of the warriors were in position because Wayne had moved more slowly than they expected; others had gone farther back to cook and still others were asleep. Wayne's artillery came up and fired canister into the area. The left wing of the Legion sent its own cavalry around the timbers while the infantry waded in among them with fixed bayonets. The militiamen dismounted and followed. Indian reinforcements running forward discovered that the others were fleeing and were carried back with them, only to meet the encircling cavalry. About a hundred white settlers and Detroit militiamen were able to block the American attack briefly, giving most of the Indians a chance to escape.

The Indians fled back to the British post, Fort Miamis. But British soldiers with fixed bayonets guarded the gate; not an Indian was permitted inside. The British commander, Major William Campbell, felt that if he offered shelter to the warriors, Wayne surely would attack the post. The Indians had to fend for themselves.

After the Battle of Fallen Timbers, which lasted about an hour and a half, Wayne had his army camp a half mile from the fort. The following day he had reconnaissance parties inspect the fort; they reported that it was strong and would be difficult to take. And Wayne in any event did not want to start a war with Britain. Neither did Major Campbell want to start one with the United States. He sent out a party headed by a captain and consisting of a sergeant, four privates, and ten fifers and drummers, to deliver a message to Wayne saying that their two countries were at peace and asking why Wayne was there.

Wayne sent back a letter asking in effect why Fort Miamis was there. Next day, with most of his army behind him, the general rode to within fifty yards of the fort; his soldiers then spread out and destroyed everything they found outside the walls, even including hay that had been cut for the garrison's horses. Campbell did not fire on them; he responded with yet another formally impolite message, Wayne replied in like manner, and Campbell once again responded in kind. Then on August 23 the Legion of the United States buried its dead with drum beat and cannon salute, and immediately afterward began the long march back to Greene Ville.

Stopping at Fort Defiance to make its defenses even stronger, Wayne sent off a message of peace to the Indians with the woman who had been captured a month earlier. He did not neglect to point out in his message that the British had failed to help the Indians at the crucial moment. After strengthening the walls at Defiance, he moved through autumn rain and snow, arriving on October 17 at the site of Harmar's defeat, near the place where the St. Mary's and St. Joseph Rivers join to form the Maumee. There he erected Fort Wayne (now the city in Indiana). Leaving six companies at that fort he proceeded on the 27th to Greene Ville, arriving on November 3.

Meanwhile the effects of the Battle of Fallen Timbers reached across the Atlantic. Chief Justice John Jay had for some months been in London, trying to negotiate British withdrawal from the border posts. He had had little success until word arrived of Wayne's victory and it was evident that the United States now had an army capable, if necessary, of advancing on Detroit itself. British statesmen became willing to talk, and soon Jay had a treaty binding the British to withdraw from their posts on American territory. That treaty was ratified by Congress on June 22, 1795.

At the same time, Wayne's peace initiative with the Indians brought results. By mid-June the tribes began to gather at Greene Ville and by mid-July Wayne was able to hold a general council. There on August 3, 1795 the Indians signed the Treaty of Greenville, ceding more than half of present-day Ohio to the United States.

In December Wayne left Greene Ville for a journey home; in the middle of February he reached Philadelphia. He was escorted into the city by three troops of the Philadelphia Light Horse, the city bells were rung in his honor, and a fifteen-gun salute boomed out. During that winter and spring he rested. By June 16 he was back at Greene Ville. On August 7 he

Fort William about 1812. From a watercolor by Robert Irvine, captain of a schooner on Lake Ontario. (Hudson's Bay Company Archives)

received Fort Miamis from the British. He arrived at Detroit on the 13th. British troops had withdrawn from the city and American troops had preceded him; his duties were mainly ceremonial and he was welcomed by the Indian tribes and by the remaining French and British inhabitants.

Wayne sent off a detachment of soldiers to Mackinac and turned over control of the region to a representative of the civil government of the Northwest Territory. He wrote to the Secretary of War, reporting that all posts on the American side of the border were now in possession of the United States. Then he sailed on the sloop *Detroit* —the first vessel to fly the American flag on the upper Great Lakes—for Presque Isle (present-day Erie, Pennsylvania), arriving on November 18. He planned to rest a few days before going on to Pittsburgh. But at Presque Isle he was stricken with his old ailment; for two weeks he lay in agonizing pain in the Presque Isle blockhouse, and there on December 15 he died—from "the Gout in his stomach."

The boundary provisions of the Jay treaty had another, delayed result. In 1804 the North West Company abandoned its fort at Grand Portage, now in United States territory, and moved to Fort William—or as it was first known, the New Fort—on the mouth of the Kaministiquia River at the northwestern corner of Lake Superior. The River Kam, as it is called for short, was the first part of another canoe route westward, a route more difficult than the one that began at Grand Portage, but one farther from United States control. The Kaministiquia had falls and rapids which caused the voyageurs to work harder—and complain more—and which required the canoes to carry smaller loads. As a partial solution, the company established a warehouse at Mountain Portage, at the upper end of the most difficult passage, where provisions were stored. Canoe brigades could then pick up their food and other necessities for the westward trip after they passed the hardest going.

Fort William was a palisaded area of several acres, in which stood a number of big, two-story, hewn-timber buildings with high, steeply pitched roofs. Some buildings, such as the powder magazine, were of stone. The fort was the field headquarters of the North West Company. To it each year came the canoe brigades from Montreal over what now was the classic route—the Ottawa River, Lake Nipissing, French River, Georgian Bay, the North Channel, Sault Ste. Marie, and the northern shore of Lake Superior. At it each summer met the partners of the North West Company. The wintering partners—the field commanders—came in from their posts throughout the north and west, to meet the Montreal partners—the agents responsible for the sales of fur abroad.

There they met, feasted, and drank in the portrait-lined Great Hall, danced, and sang. And there in lengthy meetings they hammered out the policies that governed the trade, while the cargoes of the big Montreal canoes were broken down into smaller loads which fitted into the north canoes that would carry them on from there. Also at Fort William they planned commercial moves against the Hudson's Bay Company, which brought goods by ship into Hudson Bay and then southward over shorter routes to deal with the tribes of the interior.

Relationships between the two companies varied over the years from gentlemanly to murderous. Most often they were amicable. Men of one company would carry letters for men of the other, and at Christmas the competing traders from nearby

posts would gather at one of them for dinner. But when the young and idealistic Earl of Selkirk (who said of the fur trade, "it is a business that I hate from the bottom of my heart") bought control of the Hudson's Bay Company in 1811 and the following year began to bring Scottish settlers—the crofters who had been evicted from their highland holdings—into the Red River area, thus starting to wipe out the heart of the northwestern fur country by converting it into farmland, relations between the companies approached civil war. The real outbreak between them, however, would not come until after Britain and the United States resolved the formally declared War of 1812, far to the east and south.

Led by a piper, three North West Company partners approach the wharf to welcome an arriving colleague. The parts are played by seasonal interpreters at the reconstructed Old Fort William. (Old Fort William)

4
THE WAR OF 1812

General Hull surrenders Detroit to General Brock, as shown in an old print. (Burton Historical Collection, Detroit Public Library)

By 1811 the conflict between American settlers and Indians had pushed on to Indiana Territory. The major opponents were William Henry Harrison, governor of the territory (who had been a junior officer in Wayne's army) and Tecumseh, a Shawnee chief who was organizing the Indian nations to stand against white incursion. Though a remarkable leader, Tecumseh never became as successful as Pontiac had been half a century earlier. Harrison was aware that an uprising was probably in the making. And during one of Tecumseh's absences from his headquarters at Tippecanoe on an organizing journey, his younger brother, a mystic known as the Prophet, foolishly directed an attack against a mixed force of regulars and militia under Harrison's control, thereby providing the governor with a reason for defeating the assembled warriors, destroying Tippecanoe village, and shattering the Indian confederation before it was well formed. Tecumseh and his remaining followers retreated to Amherstburg, near Fort Malden, in British territory across from Detroit.

The presence of the major Indian leader on British soil became one more irritant to Western American war hawks in the tense period just before the War of 1812. Historians still argue the reasons that the United States declared that war. Was it the traditional list of grievances against Great Britain (boarding American vessels at sea, impressing American sailors, blockading commerce) or was it the desire of the Westerners of the day—those living south of the Great Lakes—to expand northward? The foremost seafaring region of the country, New England, almost seceded from the union in its opposition to the war. The Americans who lived west of the Alleghenies, who had been steadily taking over Indian lands, and who saw in a weakly defended Canada a further opportunity for expansion, certainly influenced its declaration.

Above: Tecumseh. (From B.J. Lossing, Pictorial Field-Book of the War of 1812)

Below: William Henry Harrison, governor of Indiana Territory and then commanding general of the U.S. North Western Army during the War of 1812. (Ohio Historical Society)

The senior line officer in the U.S. Army was sixty-one-year-old Major General Henry Dearborn, appointed in January, 1812 after holding civilian political jobs for many years; his only qualification was that he had distinguished himself in the Revolutionary War. He now was given command of the Northern Department, which was to attack Montreal, Kingston, and the Niagara Peninsula. The other key commander in the Great Lakes region was sixty-year-old Brigadier General William Hull, also a Revolutionary War veteran who had spent the intervening years in political jobs, currently as governor of Michigan Territory. He commanded the North Western Army, which was to strike eastward into Canada from Detroit.

Hull accepted the appointment reluctantly. His force consisted of Ohio Volunteers, some Michigan militia, and a small force of regulars. He crossed into Canada on July 12 and issued a windy proclamation saying that he had come to emancipate the Canadians from tyranny. Some Canadians did join his force, but they were balanced by the more than a hundred Ohio men who refused to go into Canadian territory, saying they had enlisted only for service in the United States. Hull then had about twelve hundred men with whom to assault the nearby Fort Malden at Amherstburg.

Amherstburg and Fort Malden in 1813, from a watercolor by Margaret Reynolds. (Fort Malden National Historic Park)

But he decided to delay in order to float heavy artillery over from Detroit. Then he heard from friendly Indians that Fort Mackinac had been taken by the British (no one had thought to notify the American commander at that remote post that war had been declared). On August 2 Hull still was sitting on Canadian soil just across the river from Detroit, planning his attack on Fort Malden, when the paroled garrison from Mackinac reached Detroit by schooner; the Wyandot Indians living nearby, who had been allied with the Americans, promptly crossed the river and joined the British.

General Hull wrote to the governors of Ohio and Kentucky asking for reinforcements, and sent off orders telling the garrison of isolated Fort Dearborn, on the site of present-day Chicago, to withdraw to Fort Wayne. On August 6 the heavy guns were ready and Hull was about to attack Fort Malden; on August 7 he heard that British regulars from Niagara were marching to reinforce the fort—and on August 8 he retreated back to Detroit.

The British reinforcements, which did not arrive until the night of August 13, consisted of fifty regulars, two hundred and fifty militiamen, and—the most important ingredient—Major General Isaac Brock, an intelligent, bold officer who had seen extended combat service in Europe and who had considerable experience in Canada. There is a story that when Brock first met Tecumseh, the Indian leader turned to his followers and said, "This is a man." The story may be apocryphal, but the sentiment is apt.

Brock now had a total of three hundred regulars and four hundred militia, plus an indeterminate number of Indians, against Hull's four hundred regulars and eight hundred militia. On August 15 Brock sent a message to Hull demanding that he surrender. "You must be aware," he wrote, "that the numerous body of Indians who have attached themselves to

Sir Isaac Brock. In real life he was not quite the sneering figure shown in the print on page 56. From an oil portrait by J.W. L. Forster. (National Archives of Canada C7760)

my troops will be beyond control the moment the contest commences." It was a clever piece of psychological warfare; Hull refused to surrender, but he began to worry about an Indian massacre.

Hull had sent four hundred of his best militia south to meet a supply train. He placed his remaining militia to guard the landward side of the fort and kept his regulars inside it. He put no guards at the narrowest part of the river, the logical crossing place, three miles below Detroit. That night about six hundred Indians crossed there. Early on August 16, Brock himself crossed with seven hundred soldiers and landed without opposition. He then advanced on Detroit. Many of his militiamen wore old red coats borrowed from the British regulars, and Brock had the sections advance with double the normal distance between them. From the walls of the fort at Detroit the little force looked like a formidable army. The Michigan militia immediately deserted their posts. British artillery on the far side of the river began to toss shells into the fort. Without firing a shot, Hull surrendered.

S oon after the outbreak of war, the British forces at the ramshackle fort on St. Joseph's Island (to which the British had withdrawn when they turned over Mackinac to the Americans) moved toward American-held Mackinac Island. On the night

Fort St. Joseph was constructed by the British when they withdrew from Fort Mackinac in 1796, following Anthony Wayne's campaign that established the U.S. claim to that post. Here is St. Joseph, which was only forty-five miles from Mackinac, as it appeared in 1804. At the beginning of the war of 1812 the British garrison here moved back to Mackinac and recaptured that fort, whose commander had not been told by his government that they were declaring war. Sketch by Edward Walsh. (William L. Clements Library)

Prepared under direction of D.O.Drennan Agent Chicago Hist.Soc.

Copyrighted, 1897 by Geo. H. Fergus.

Chas. H. Durand
Wash" D.C. Sep 1897

of July 16 the British landed at a sheltered place on the shore of the island and next morning were in position on the hill above the fort with cannon and muskets aimed down into it. Lieutenant Porter Hanks, the American commander who never had been warned by his own government that they were declaring war, had little alternative but to surrender.

As word spread of the British victory at Mackinac, the Indians began to gather around other American forts. They gathered at what now is Chicago near Fort Dearborn, where Captain Nathan Heald commanded the small garrison of about fifty men. In response to the order from General Hull to withdraw to Fort Wayne, he first distributed much trade goods to the Indians in return for promises of safe conduct, and then set out on the morning of August 15 with his soldiers, a handfull of local settlers and militia, and their families. At the head of the column was Captain William Wells, a veteran Indian fighter who had served under Anthony Wayne; he had come from Fort Wayne with thirty friendly Miami braves to lead the way back. The garrison did not trust the Indians; prophetically the fifes and drums played a funeral march as they started out.

The hostile Indians waited in ambush behind some nearby sand dunes. Wells saw them and gave the alarm, just before an attack that killed about half the regulars. The others rallied

Fort Dearborn, at the present site of Chicago. Modern drawing made by Charles H. Durand from the original plans. (Chicago Historical Society)

and charged them, driving them back across the dunes—but in the process became separated from the baggage train where most of the women and children rode. The Chicago militia guarded that part of the column. Militia and families were quickly overwhelmed and most of them slaughtered. In the fight Wells was killed, scalped, and his body was beheaded. His Miami Indians had long since fled. The remaining soldiers held a parley in which the hostile Indians promised that if the Americans surrendered none of them would be harmed. They agreed, and as they were led back to the fort they passed the baggage train where they saw the women and children "lying naked with principally all their heads off."

Once back at the fort, the Indians soon began to torture and kill their captives. The few survivors were then taken away in all directions after the departing bands of Indians had burned the fort. Both Captain and Mrs. Heald were badly wounded, but survived the battle, ending it in the hands of different groups of Indians. The family of John Kinzie, a nearby fur trader the Indians considered a neutral, waited in a boat near the shore in case they too had to flee. Mrs. Kinzie saw Mrs. Heald's predicament and sent one of her husband's clerks to trade an old mule and some whiskey to the band holding her, so that they would transfer her to the one that held her husband. Eventually the Healds escaped and after a three-hundred-mile voyage in a canoe made their way to Mackinac. There Captain Roberts, the British commander, gave them a small sailboat and sent them on to Detroit.

B y the end of September 1812 there was a respectable build-up of American strength along the Niagara frontier. Major General Stephen Van Rensselaer, a successful Albany politician who had been commissioned in the New York militia, commanded nine hundred regulars and twenty-six hundred and fifty militia, centered about Lewiston, near Fort Niagara on the American side of the river. Brigadier General Alexander Smyth, a lawyer who had been commissioned a few years earlier in the regular service, had sixteen hundred and fifty regulars at Buffalo.

On the night of October 10, Van Rensselaer made an abortive attempt to cross the Niagara River and attack Queenston, the small Canadian town opposite Lewiston. His men had had no previous experience in handling boats, several of the boats had no oars, and a heavy rain dampened everyone's spirits. The

river crossing was postponed until early morning of the 13th. At that time three hundred militia and three hundred regulars crossed into Canada. The militia were soon pinned down by British fire coming from the village of Queenston, but the regulars, under Captain John Wool, found their way up a trail leading to the top of Queenston Heights, three hundred and fifty feet above the river.

The Battle of Queenston Heights, October 1812. This drawing by Major James Dennis shows a composite of events. (National Archives of Canada C276)

General Brock, who had returned from Detroit to his headquarters at Fort George, across the river from the American-held Fort Niagara, was awakened by the attack. As soon as he was certain of its direction, he mounted his horse Alfred and galloped toward it. At Queenston, he ordered the infantry company stationed on the Heights to come down into the village to help a company there that was holding off the militia attack. He was of course unaware that Captain Wool had found a path from the river and was leading his U.S. regulars up to the top of the Heights, and his experience at Detroit may have led him to underestimate the Americans. In any event, it was a fatal decision. Brock himself rode to the top and dismounted at a position where one of his small cannon was emplaced. It was a good observation post and he stood there, looking down on the battlefield.

Without warning, the U.S. regulars came over the crest and charged down on the gun position from behind. The artillerymen spiked their gun and they and Brock went down the hill on the double, Brock on foot and leading his horse. In the village below he rallied about two hundred men and started them back up the steep slope to the Heights. The brilliant uniform of a major general, with a scarf Tecumseh had given him tied around the throat, made Brock a perfect target. As the small force advanced up hill he was shot in the wrist, but continued to push forward. Then he was shot in the chest. The shot killed him on the spot. The counterattack faltered, then retreated back down the slope.

An aide to Brock, Colonel John Macdonell, arrived with two more militia companies, renewed the attack, and reached the abandoned gun position on the heights. Macdonell was killed at about that point. On the U.S. side Captain Wool was seriously wounded, but the Americans were reinforced and Colonel Winfield Scott, another young American regular, took over from Wool. Scott, six feet five inches tall and dressed in full uniform, was an imposing figure (and also a good target, though he was never hit). The Americans rallied. Once more the British and Canadians retreated down the hill.

But the militiamen on the New York side of the river, waiting their turn to be ferried across to the battlefield, now refused to get into the boats. Seeing and hearing the battle, they suddenly decided that they were legally bound to serve only in the United States. The three hundred and fifty U.S. regulars and two hundred and fifty militiamen defending the heights now received neither reinforcements nor fresh ammunition.

On the British side, Major General Roger Shaeffe arrived with about three hundred regulars and two hundred and fifty militiamen drawn from points farther west. Led by Indians, Shaeffe followed a path that took his force up to the Heights some distance to the west of the American position. As he went he gathered in another hundred regulars and more Indians, the latter bringing his Indian total to about three hundred. At three in the afternoon the British attacked the Americans on the flank, taking them by complete surprise. The white cravat of Captain Totten, one of Winfield Scott's subordinates, stuck on the point of Scott's sword, was their flag of surrender.

During this action the United States forces suffered three hundred casualties and 958 taken prisoner. The British had about ninety casualties and twenty-one missing. The British also were in the difficult position of having almost as many prisoners as soldiers. Van Rensselaer asked for a three-day armistice, to which Shaeffe agreed; Van Rensselaer then submitted his resignation to Dearborn, who accepted it and ordered General Smyth to take command on the Niagara frontier. Smyth made two feeble attempts to cross the river, then took leave to visit his family and never came back to duty.

Meanwhile, early in October, Captain Isaac Chauncey of the U.S. Navy arrived at Sackets Harbor on Lake Ontario and began to establish an American naval squadron there, buying several merchant vessels for immediate conversion to fighting ships and beginning construction of some true warships. The only naval vessel there when Chauncey arrived was the U.S. brig *Oneida*.

The British already had on Lake Ontario a motley collection of small vessels that had belonged to the colonial government's transport and patrol service, the Provincial Marine. Early in November Chauncey sailed with the *Oneida* and his squadron of newly armed schooners, discovered the small British vessel *Royal George*, and chased her into the Canadian harbor of Kingston, at the eastern end of the lake. There, however, fire from shore batteries and a blockhouse under construction on Point Henry drove him off. As a naval action it did not amount to much, but it did establish that Chauncey now controlled the lake.

Next spring, in April 1813, Chauncey and General Dearborn launched an attack against the town of York (present-day Toronto) at the western end of Lake Ontario. Fourteen vessels carrying seventeen hundred regular soldiers under Dearborn arrived at York on April 26. There had been some construc-

Southeast view of Sackets Harbor, American naval base and military post on Lake Ontario. The British attacked here in 1813, but were driven off. This engraving by W. Strickland was published in 1815, but probably shows the harbor and harbor defenses as they were during the war. (New York Public Library)

South east view of Sacketts harbour.

tion of defenses there at Fort York, but they were not far advanced. Three artillery batteries were set up along the shore, but their heaviest guns were old and in poor condition. A stone powder magazine stood near the shoreline, and a few sketchy earthworks around it outlined the fort that was not yet completed.

In command of these British defenses at York was Major General Shaeffe, who had won the final battle after Brock's death at Queenston Heights. He had been sick during the winter, however, and here he had no more than seven hundred men, about half of them local militia. He kept most of his force inside the unfinished fort, waiting for the proper moment to counterattack the invaders. The landing began about eight in the morning of the 26th and soon four companies of U.S. infantry were ashore. With them came Brigadier General Zebulon Pike, second in command of the American military force.

Here in 1813 is the British block-house on Point Henry that protected the Kingston Naval base. The fortifications would be greatly enlarged during the war. From a drawing by Capt. Viger, Canadian Voltigeurs. (Parks of the St. Lawrence)

The British counterattack, as a result of confusion on the part of the defenders, was made by only one company, the grenadiers of the King's Regiment, a picked company of one of the best British regiments. Their bayonet charge reached the beach; one American officer stepping from a boat was bayoneted in the shoulder. But it was one company against four, with more Americans landing; the grenadiers, their com-

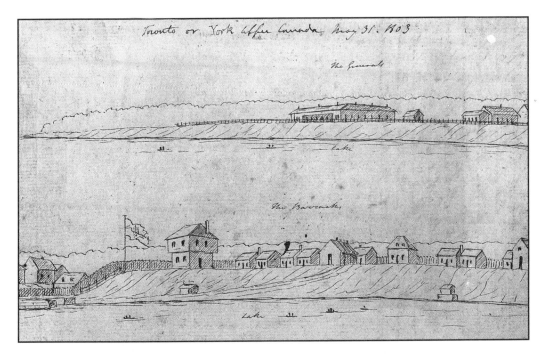

The fort at York (present-day Toronto) shown here in 1803 was little changed in April 1813 when the Americans captured it. From a sketch by Lt. Sempronius Stretton. (National Archives of Canada C14822)

pany commander dead and many others dead or wounded were forced to retreat toward the town. General Shaeffe had lost control of his command; three other companies arrived piecemeal on the battlefield and were defeated one at a time.

The American force advanced along the beach with the support of naval gunfire from Chauncey's ships. Pike's field guns were landed and opened fire on the British positions. The local militia began to fade away from the defensive works. Shaeffe decided that he had to withdraw his regulars. Leaving the flag flying over the fort, he marched his men away toward Kingston, advising the militia commanders to make contact with the Americans and get the best terms they could. He sent men to set fire to a warship under construction in the harbor and to blow up the powder magazine.

By then the Americans were at the edge of the fort. Because its flag was still flying they thought it still was garrisoned—which of course was Shaeffe's reason for leaving the flag there. General Pike was questioning a captured British sergeant when the stone magazine blew up. One witness said that the building rose slowly, assuming the shape of a vast balloon; then out of the balloon-shaped cloud huge stones and wooden beams began to rain down on the nearby Americans. Pike's back and chest were crushed, twenty-eight of his men were killed outright, and over two hundred were wounded.

Pike was carried out to Chauncey's flagship, the new U.S.S. *Madison*, where he died. General Dearborn landed and took personal command ashore. The Americans occupied the town for five days. When they sailed away they burned what was left of the buildings in the fort. The day before, someone also burned the small brick parliament buildings in town; there have been arguments ever since as to who did it, but the best theory seems to be that it was the unauthorized work of a group of U.S. seamen.

Farther west, on Lake Erie, the command of American forces had passed to William Henry Harrison, now commissioned a brigadier general of regulars. Harrison planned to gather an army near the rapids of the Maumee River and to move against Detroit from there. In January 1813 one of his subordinate commanders, General James Winchester, arrived at the rapids and began to build an armed camp. Soon after his arrival two Frenchmen from the village of River Raisin (also called Frenchtown because of the background of its inhabitants), a settlement halfway between the mouth of the Maumee and Detroit, came to Winchester and told him that a small group of Indians and British soldiers at that place guarded three thousand barrels of flour and a considerable amount of corn and wheat intended for the British garrison at Fort Malden. On the heels of these men came others to say that the British had discovered their friendship for the Americans and were going to destroy their village.

Winchester had orders from Harrison to stay at his camp until the full army was assembled and ready to move on Detroit, but he felt that he had to act now. He sent about seven hundred men toward the River Raisin under Colonel William Lewis, who handily defeated the British and Indians there and who then sent back to Winchester asking for reinforcements to hold the place. Winchester sent three hundred regulars under Colonel Samuel Wells, and also proceeded by carriage himself, arriving at the village even before the reinforcements got there. Wells, when he arrived, pointed out to Winchester that the troops were in a highly exposed position, and also suggested that scouts be sent out to learn what the British were doing. Winchester, no doubt weary from his long carriage ride over bad roads, said that tomorrow would be time enough to take care of these things, and went off to stay in the comfortable home of one of the community leaders, more than a mile away from his soldiers.

Colonel Henry Procter, who had succeeded General Brock as British commander at Detroit, that night led six hundred soldiers and six hundred Indians against the Americans, attacking before dawn. Wells's regulars formed behind a picket fence and were able to kill or wound 185 of the attackers. The American militia, however, were taken by surprise in the open and quickly overcome. In the general confusion, Winchester was captured by Chief Roundhead, who took him to Procter. The British commander persuaded the shaken Winchester that he should order his regulars to surrender, supposedly to avoid a massacre by the Indians. The fighting over, Procter withdrew to Fort Malden, taking his prisoners with him, except for sixty-four wounded Americans he left at River Raisin, intending to send sleds to get them the next day. That night about two hundred of the Indians returned and massacred thirty of the wounded men.

Harrison, his campaign against Detroit aborted by Winchester's blundering, then began to build Fort Meigs, named for Governor Return J. Meigs of Ohio, near the rapids of the Maumee. It stood on high bluffs on the south side of the river, looking across to the flat land on the north side where Wayne had fought the Battle of Fallen Timbers. Harrison continued to plan a campaign to retake Detroit, but had to release his restive Kentucky militia, who demanded to go home if they were not going to fight immediately. Harrison then organized a raid on Fort Malden across the ice of Lake Erie and the Detroit River, but was forced to cancel it after the raiders, travelling in sleighs, discovered open water ahead of them. Thinking that same condition would prevent any British attack, he took time to visit Cincinnati in order to see his family and to raise more soldiers.

But in late March it became evident that Procter was indeed planning an attack, and Harrison quickly returned to Fort Meigs. Procter now had been made brigadier general and Harrison had been made major general. On April 28 a flotilla of small vessels and large boats landed a British force of about a thousand soldiers and twelve hundred Indians at the mouth of the Maumee River. Procter made his headquarters at the site of old Fort Miamis, about two miles downriver on the opposite side. By May 1 his artillery batteries opened fire on Fort Meigs and his Indians, led by Tecumseh, surrounded it.

A brigade of twelve hundred Kentucky militia under General Green Clay was coming to reinforce the garrison, however. The British and Indian siege was so loosely organized that Clay was able to get messages in to Harrison and together they planned a coordinated attack. On May 5, eight hundred of the Kentuckians under Colonel William Dudley (described by one diarist as "a man alike ignorant and rash, and who had never heard a hostile gun") attacked and captured the batteries on the far side of the river. They spiked some of the guns while soldiers from the fort sallied out and took the battery on the south bank. But then, instead of finishing their work and returning by boat to the fort as planned, the Kentucky militia let themselves be drawn farther into the woods by the retreating Indians. The British and Indians then struck with a swift counterattack. Less than a hundred Americans got back across the river; the others were either taken prisoner or killed in battle or later by the Indians. (A British officer who tried to stop the slaughter of the prisoners was shot down, but Tecumseh, coming on the scene in violent anger, disbursed his murderous followers.)

Fort Malden at Amhertsburg, on the Canadian side of the Detroit River, in 1823. (National Archives of Canada C 83305)

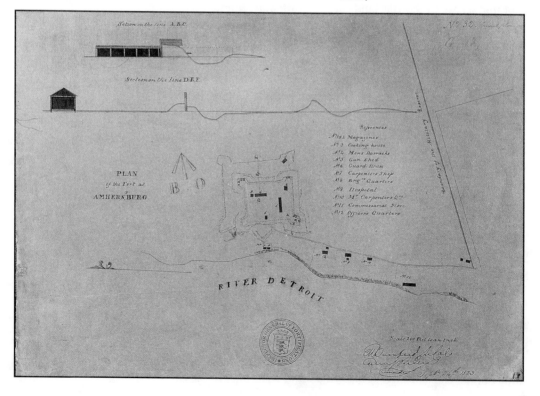

Immediately after the action Procter's militiamen and Indians began to drift away, so that by May 9 he had in addition to his regulars only a handful of militia and a few loyal Indians under Tecumseh. He abandoned the siege, loaded his cannon on the boats, and went back to Fort Malden.

On the 11th, Harrison turned over command of the fort to General Clay and travelled to Sandusky to see to the defenses of that region, especially of the supply depot located on the Sandusky River. He went on to Cleveland, then headed south to Franklinton (present-day Columbus) where he made his headquarters while he raised reinforcements and tried to persuade Governor Meigs of the need for more forts along Lake Erie.

By mid-July Procter's provisions had run low and he decided to raid Harrison's lightly guarded supply depot at Lower Sandusky. But Tecumseh insisted that instead he attack Fort Meigs again. Procter was afraid of losing the support of the Indians, and so he agreed. On July 20 he reached Fort Meigs with three hundred regulars and three thousand Indians. Tecumseh planned to draw the Americans out of the fort by staging, with much shooting and yelling, a sham battle half a mile in rear of the fort, as though the Indians were attacking a body of reinforcements coming into Fort Meigs. But the garrison realized it was a trick and did not respond.

Procter decided against making an assault and on the 28th moved along the shore toward his original goal at Sandusky. Only two or three hundred of the Indians remained with him, but they insisted now on attacking the small Fort Stephenson, which guarded the passage upriver to the depot, rather than bypassing the fort as Procter intended. Once more, Procter let his judgement be overruled and consented to the attack.

Harrison had told Major George Croghan (a nephew of George Rogers Clark) who commanded Fort Stephenson, that in the event of an attack by a superior force he should withdraw. Croghan, however, stood firm with his hundred-and-sixty regulars and a single cannon. Procter's small field guns made little impression on the stockaded fort, so he determined on an assault. The defenders responded with heavy rifle fire and scrap iron fired from their one cannon. By the time the British had ninety-six casualties and the Indians had disappeared from the scene entirely, Procter called off the attack and limped home.

But other forces were moving to resolve the conflict on Lake Erie. President Madison had long since decided that as long as the British controlled the lake and were able to move

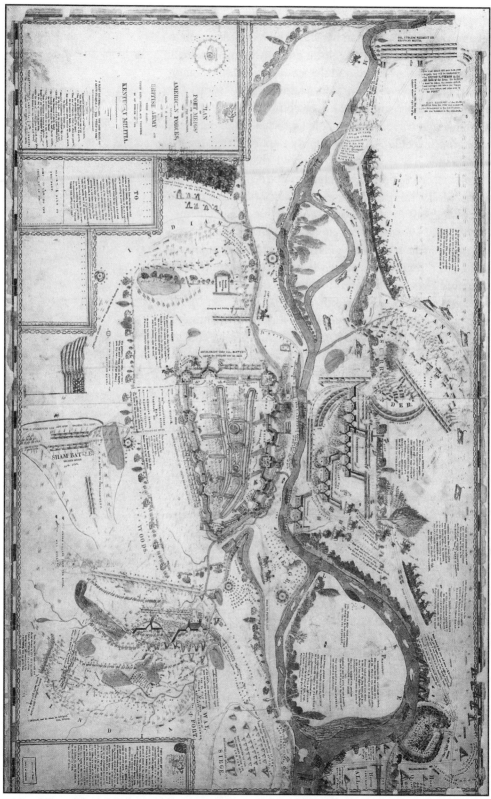

Map of Fort Meigs and vicinity by Capt. William Sebree of the Kentucky Militia. The fort itself is in the center; around it are shown all the various activities that took place. The overall map is drawn in three different scales. (Library of Congress 317852)

forces over it almost at will, the Americans could not retake Detroit. The British vessels of the Provincial Marine were poor warships, but the Americans had no ships at all. As a result, early in 1813 the young naval officer Master Commandant Oliver Hazard Perry (whose rank was equal to that of a navy commander today) made the long trip overland and arrived at Presque Isle to build an American naval squadron on the lake. Shortly afterward Lieutenant Robert Barclay of the Royal Navy arrived on the British side, at Amherstburg near Fort Malden, to form a British squadron.

By early September Procter—now a major general—having failed to capture Harrison's supplies, was in a desperate situation. He had to feed not only his own people, but also a large number of Indian warriors and their families who had attached themselves to him—a total of more than fourteen thousand people. Perry's squadron was now on the lake, intercepting any British supplies that were sent over it. On September 5 Procter had only two or three days' rations left for this mass of people. He consulted with Barclay, and they decided that Barclay's squadron, though short of men and supplies, had to go out and fight Perry's. The two squadrons met on September 10, near the western end of the lake.

At the end of the Battle of Lake Erie, Perry sent his famous victory message to Harrison: "We have met the enemy and They are ours."

On September 20, Perry's ships and a fleet of small boats began to embark Harrison's forty-five hundred soldiers to carry them across the lake, except for a regiment of Kentucky cavalry that proceeded around the lake toward Detroit. On the afternoon of the 27th the American force landed, to find that General Procter had pulled back his men from Fort Malden and was retreating inland. Tecumseh was bitter at the retreat, but agreed to go for a way with the British forces. His devoted followers went with him. Most of the Indians, however, who had been contented consumers of British rations, now took themselves elsewhere.

Harrison, after leaving soldiers to garrison Detroit and Fort Malden, had something more than three thousand men with whom to pursue the British. By October 1 the regiment of Kentucky cavalry, which had crossed at Detroit, also caught up with Harrison's force. Procter, who had his family with him, retreated eastward along the Thames River faster than his own men, with the purpose—or on the pretext of—looking for a good place to make a stand. By October 5 the Americans were hot on the heels of the British and Procter had to find a place to stop and fight. He hastily chose a position, placing his regulars in two lines across the road and in the woods on either side of it, with the river on his left flank and the Indians in a strong natural position in a swamp on his right.

Harrison attacked with Colonel Richard Johnson's Kentucky cavalry in the center and held back his left flank from contact with the Indians in the swamp. The tired British soldiers, with scant breastworks to protect them, only got off a scattered fire before the Kentuckians had ridden over them and were rounding them up in small groups as prisoners. Johnson then had his men dismount and attack the Indians in the swamp. The bloodiest kind of hand-to-hand frontier fighting resulted, and only after a vicious battle, during which Tecumseh was killed, did the Indians flee from their position.

The greatest tragedy at the Battle of the Thames was the death of that remarkable man Tecumseh. Harrison, who first had destroyed his hopes at Tippecanoe, now had finished him. But even in 1813 it was evident that his impossible dream of turning the clock back on white settlement could never be realized. This brave ending may have been the best one for him.

Fort George as seen from Fort Niagara, 1812. Note Fort Niagara's American flag at upper right. Legend has it that Fort Niagara officers were dinner guests at Fort George when word arrived that war had been declared; the British officers insisted that the Americans finish the meal before escorting them politely back to their boats and saying goodbye. (National Archives of Canada C26)

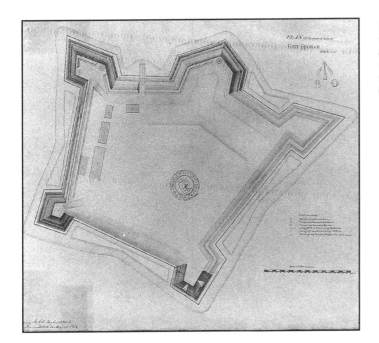

Plan of Fort George, 1814. By this time, the British had considerably changed its shape from what it was at the beginning of the war. (National Archives of Canada C30389)

There was action on Lake Ontario that summer of 1813, but it was far less decisive. Toward the end of May, Chauncey's squadron shelled Fort George on the Canadian side of the Niagara River, on the 27th landing three brigades of militia and some regulars under Colonel Winfield Scott (who had been exchanged as a prisoner of war). Rather than letting himself be bottled up in the relatively weak fort, Brigadier General John Vincent, commanding the small British force, moved back toward the western end of the lake. The Americans took over the fort, but were slow and ineffectual in pursuing the British.

In July, the government at Washington decided that the time had come to put Major General Dearborn out to pasture. In his place they appointed Major General James Wilkinson, of whom it has been said that he never won a battle or lost a court of inquiry. (The high point of his career was probably his association with Aaron Burr in the attempt to detach Louisiana from the United States.) Wilkinson turned his attention to the St. Lawrence and Lake Champlain regions, where he fared so badly—not entirely through his own fault—that early in 1814 he asked for a court of inquiry to rule on the conduct of this campaign. His request was granted and he never returned to active service, though once again he won an acquittal.

When Wilkinson took his force down the St. Lawrence, he left the U.S. naval base at Sackets Harbor virtually unprotected. A brigade of regulars which had recently been moved to the Niagara region from Detroit was therefore sent on to garrison Sackets Harbor. This left a brigade of New York militia under General George McClure to hold the entire Niagara frontier. McClure, whose headquarters was at Fort George on the Brit-

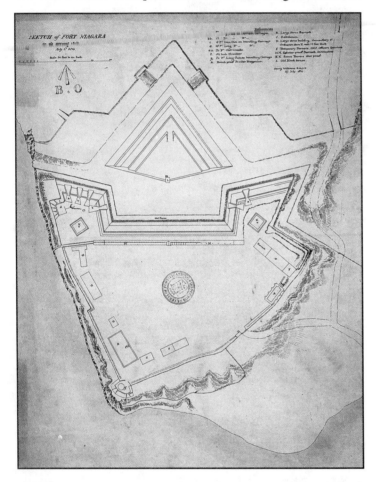

Plan of Fort Niagara, made by the British in 1814. (National Archives of Canada C15157)

ish side of the Niagara River, found himself with a rapidly dwindling force of militiamen whose terms of service were up and who insisted on going home. By December 10 he had only about a hundred men. And so, when he learned that a larger British force was approaching, he withdrew across the river to the much stronger Fort Niagara.

But McClure did one other thing. He burned the Canadian town of Newark (now Niagara-on-the-Lake), turning the inhabitants out of their houses on short notice on a cold winter

night and leaving them to fend for themselves. The United States government quickly notified Sir George Prevost, the British commander in Canada, that McClure's action was "unauthorized by the American government and abhorrent to every American feeling," but the excuse had been provided for the British to burn several American towns in the vicinity, and to burn Washington the following year.

The oncoming British force, under Colonel John Murray, on December 19 crossed the Niagara River before dawn. By then, McClure had gone on to Buffalo, leaving a Captain Leonard in command at Fort Niagara. That night Leonard went home to his family in a house three miles away. The gate of the strong fort stood open. The attackers bayoneted the few American sentries and without firing a shot rushed the main gate and took the fort. It remained in British hands for the rest of the war. Soon after it was captured, British troops and Indians were busily at work burning the American villages of Lewiston, Black Rock, and Buffalo. (And by then, General McClure, who had begun the burning, had taken himself well inland away from the border.)

B ecause Wilkinson was otherwise engaged, little more happened around Lake Ontario until on May 6, 1814, a British squadron under Sir James Yeo, who had built up a considerable naval force on the lake, landed infantry, marines, and seamen to attack what generally was called Fort Oswego—more properly, old Fort Ontario at Oswego. The small American

Fort Niagara as seen from the Canadian side of the Niagara River at Newark (present day Niagara-on-the-Lake). From an engraving dated 1814; but as the British held the fort all during that year, the American flag shows that the original drawing was made at an earlier time. (National Archives of Canada C4455)

force there was composed mostly of artillerymen who had recently arrived at the semi-abandoned fort after a forced march, to repair the guns and patch up the fortifications.

After landing, the British formed in two columns and advanced up the steep hill toward the fort. The 290 Americans met the British attack with musket and cannon fire, killing 18 and wounding 73 of the attackers; then as the British climbed the walls the Americans fell back in good order, first to the far side of the fort, then outside the walls, Colonel Mitchell, their commander, then withdrew his men about twelve miles inland

to Oswego Falls, where there was a large quantity of naval stores waiting to be moved to the U.S. naval base at Sackets Harbor. Mitchell prepared for a last-ditch defense of the stores, but as it turned out the British did not know that they were there and wasted no time in pursuing the small body of Americans. Instead they loaded into the several schooners they had captured in the harbor some 2,400 barrels of flour and other foodstuffs, seven long guns, and various ordnance supplies. On the 7th they sailed away.

The British attack on Oswego, 1814. From a drawing by Lt. John Hewett of the Royal Marines, the hero of the battle who climbed the flagpole at Fort Ontario and pulled down the American flag nailed there, after two other men had been shot down attempting it. Understandably, the flagpole seems very high. (National Archives of Canada C793)

T hat spring Jacob Brown—a good militia officer now commissioned a major general of regulars—was put in command of a force of about thirty-five hundred men. (The secretary of war had planned for him to have eight thousand, but somehow had failed to provide them.) Some of the fiercest battles of the war were about to take place along the Niagara Frontier, anchored at its southern end by Fort Erie and at its northern by Forts George and Niagara. Under Brown were Brigadier Generals Eleazer Ripley and Winfield Scott of the regulars and Peter B. Porter of the Pennsylvania militia. On July 3 Brown crossed the Niagara River above the falls and easily took British Fort Erie, which stands on the Canadian side, opposite Buffalo, at the place where Lake Erie flows into the river. Moving southward along the Canadian side of the river, he met at Chippewa a British force of about eighteen hundred commanded by Major General Phineas Riall. Riall eagerly attacked Winfield Scott's brigade, thinking it was one more group of American amateurs, and in the resulting Battle of Chippewa was, to his astonishment, driven back. A cherished tradition of the U.S. Army is Riall's reputed exclamation, "Those are regulars, by God!" They were. As the Americans advanced he withdrew to Fort George, remaining there while Brown fortified Queenston Heights looking down on him.

According to plan, Chauncey was now to bring supplies and reinforcements over Lake Ontario to Brown. Instead, the American naval commander found reasons to stay at Sackets Harbor, refusing even to intercept British vessels carrying supplies up the lake to York, where Lieutenant General Gordon Drummond was assembling another force to move against Brown. (The close and effective inter-service coordination between Perry and Harrison on Lake Erie was seldom approached on Lake Ontario.) Under the circumstances, Brown withdrew to Chippewa again, hoping to get some supplies across the Niagara River from the small Fort Schlosser on the American side. As Brown moved back, Riall sent out a screening force of about a thousand regulars which took up position on a hill a mile or so west of Niagara Falls, near a road called Lundy's Lane.

Then Drummond came in from York with a regiment of British regulars. After conferring with Riall he decided to send five hundred soldiers and Indians from Fort Niagara along the American side of the river to attack Lewiston, while the regular regiment moved to help Riall. Brown learned of the threat to Lewiston, which would also endanger his supply base at Fort Schlosser, and decided to advance again toward Queenston, thus putting pressure on the British that might cause them to pull back the force moving toward Lewiston. He did not know that that thrust had already been cancelled and that the five hundred had returned to the vicinity of Queenston;

some of them were sent to Fort George, others were attached to Colonel Joseph Morrison's regiment of regulars that was just moving to join Riall's men already in position at Lundy's Lane.

Winfield Scott made a hasty reconnaissance of Lundy's Lane in the late afternoon of July 26. He decided that he was facing a roughly equal number of British troops, and moved his brigade into line opposite them. Drummond arrived on the field soon afterward and formed by what then was a total of about sixteen hundred soldiers into line on the slope of the hill opposite Scott, placing his artillery to support them.

At 6:00 p.m. the Americans attacked, drove back the left of the British line, and captured the seriously wounded General Riall. Repeated American attacks—they even reached and bayoneted the British artillerymen as they loaded their guns—failed to move back the British center, however. Each attack

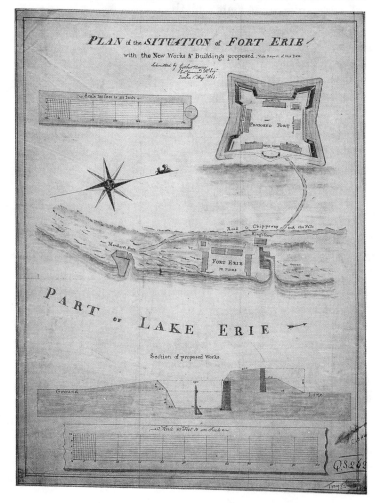

When the War of 1812 began, the proposed works in this 1803 plan of Fort Erie had not been completed. The rear of the fort was still open to attack and was protected only by a palisade. During the war it was held first by one side, then by the other. Toward the end of the war, held by the Americans and surrounded by the British, it was the site of the only true seige of the war. (National Archives of Canada C15061)

was repulsed. At 9:00 p.m. Ripley and Porter arrived with their brigades; by then Scott's brigade had been reduced to half its original strength. Ripley moved his men into battle and the British began to waver—but then they too received reinforcements of an additional twelve hundred regulars and militia. The battle continued into darkness, becoming more and more confused.

Gate to the restored Fort Erie as seen today. (Photo by the author)

By midnight both Brown and Scott had been seriously wounded and Ripley was in command. Both sides were close to exhaustion. It seemed to be a stalemate. Finally it was Ripley who drew back. The next morning he continued his retreat, abandoning or destroying a quantity of supplies and withdrawing into Fort Erie. He intended to continue right on across the river to the American side, but the wounded Brown intervened. Fort Erie was not strongly fortified, and the Americans set to work building earthworks and improving it. Until Brown recovered, Brigadier General Edmund Gaines was moved from Sackets Harbor to take command. On August 3 Drummond, having put his weary British forces in some order, arrived at Fort Erie with about three thousand men and placed it under siege.

On the 13th and 14th of August the British carried out an extensive bombardment of the fort and on the 15th they assaulted it. Most of the attackers were unable to get into the fort and one group who did so by wading along the shore was captured. But six hundred men did take the northeastern bastion. They were unable to reach the fort itself, however, despite repeated efforts. Then the powder magazine near the bastion exploded, killing or injuring a number of them, and the remainder pulled back. The British suffered 57 killed, 309 wounded, and 539 missing or captured; the Americans had only 84 killed or wounded.

On August 28 a British shell exploded in the quarters of General Gaines, wounding him seriously. General Brown, not yet fully recovered from his own wounds, came back to take command. The British had been setting up a line of siege guns to batter the fort, and Brown decided on a sortie to destroy them. He brought a thousand volunteers from the New York militia across the river into the fort to help.

There was a thick woods near the flank and rear of one of the British batteries. The Americans cleared a path through the forest to this point without being discovered. It had rained steadily during most of the siege; now under cover of a heavy downpour at 3:00 p.m. on September 16, about sixteen hundred American soldiers boiled out of the woods and overran two of the batteries, destroying the guns and blowing up the magazines. As they attacked the remaining third battery, however, a strong force arrived from the main British camp some distance away and after a brisk clash the Americans withdrew into the fort again, having destroyed half of the heavy British guns and their ammunition.

Drummond, discouraged by the American success and by the growing sickness within his own force, which was living without tents in rain and mud, gave up the siege and marched away.

Farther west on the Great Lakes that summer of 1814, the British still held Fort Mackinac, now commanded by Colonel Robert McDouall of the Royal Newfoundland Regiment. One of the first things McDouall had done when he assumed command was to build a blockhouse on the height of land behind the fort—that same height that had enabled the British to capture it.

On July 26 a squadron of five U.S. ships carrying seven hundred U.S. soldiers arrived off Mackinac, planning to assault the fort. The landing force was commanded by twenty-two-year-old George Croghan, now a lieutenant colonel—the same man who held off Procter at Fort Stephenson. Here he discovered that this fort stood so high that the naval guns could not be elevated to fire on it; thus the soldiers would have no support from the ships if they stormed the walls.

After futilely shelling the fort for two days—the shells all landed in the vegetable gardens on the open ground below—the squadron pulled back out to sea in a growing fog, which lasted a full week. Then as the weather cleared they came in at the western, low end of the island, as the British had done in 1812. After heavy bombardment of the area by the naval guns, the soldiers landed. Led by Major Andrew Holmes, they worked their way through dense woods in which lurked hostile Indians, and over a ridge into the flat, open clearing of Dousman's farm.

Instead of letting himself be penned up in the fort, McDouall, who knew his ground well, placed his small force behind low breastworks at the opposite side of the clearing. In addition to their muskets and rifles they manned two field guns. As the Americans came into the open the British had ideal targets; they killed thirteen including Holmes and two other officers, and wounded fifty-one.

Croghan pulled his men back into the woods and down to the beach. There they climbed into the boats and rowed back to their ships. The next day the Americans sailed away. Mackinac remained firmly in British hands.

After the War of 1812 the British once again turned Fort Mackinac over to the Americans in July, 1815 and moved to this new post constructed on Drummond Island. The island appeared to be safely on the Canadian side of the new border, which surely would follow the main channel. The border did not, however; the line drawn by the boundary commission put the island on the American side, and the garrison had to move once more. Here is the island post in 1820. (From John Bigsby, *The Shoe and Canoe*, National Archives of Canada C 11665)

The military part of Collier's Harb.ᵣ Drummond's I.ᵈ.   Commandon.ᵗˢ House. Barracks.

SENTINELS OF THE GREAT LAKES

FORT HOWARD
1818

 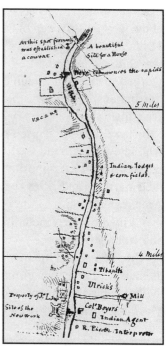

Fort Howard at Green Bay, established by the U.S. after the War of 1812. These sketches show the fort and its environs in 1818. (U.S. National Archives 111-SC-96749-1)

FORT HENRY
1819

Fort Henry at Kingston as it was expanded during the War of 1812. Throughout the history of cannons, officers knew that guns in a properly armed fort could be larger and more effective than any on shipboard. Wartime problems considerably limited Fort Henry's armament, but the fort was respected perhaps more than necessary and was never attacked. (From John Bigsby, *The Shoe and Canoe*, National Archives of Canada C 11657)

FORT MISSISSAUGA

1814

A small fort without bastions, Fort Mississauga was shaped as a slightly lopsided star. This plan, made when the fort was built at the end of the War of 1812, does not show all of the structures that eventually were inside its walls. (National Archives of Canada NMC 23031)

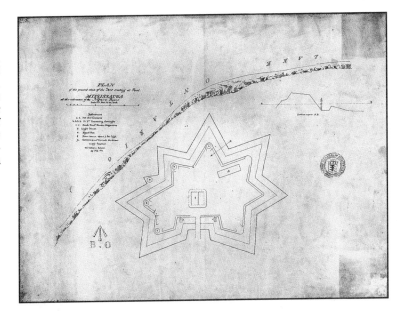

FORT YORK

1821

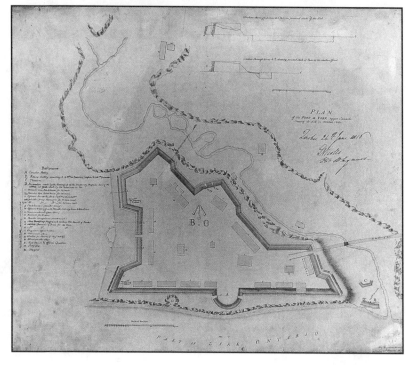

Above: This picture of Fort York, by John Elliot Woolford in 1821, shows how the fort dominated the lakeshore and the surrounding terrain. (National Archives of Canada C 99558)

Left: After the war of 1812 the British strengthened several of their forts. Here is the plan of Fort York (at present-day Toronto) as it was in 1816. (National Archives of Canada C35109)

1816

FORT BRADY

1822

Right: The Americans constructed Fort Brady at Sault Ste. Marie, or as this plan of the first cantonment there calls it, "The Sault of St. Marys." The fort was built almost entirely by the 250 soldiers who arrived to man it. The region was still pioneer country, and a local resident wrote, "Their Buildings are large well finished inside better than any we could boast of at the Sault." (U.S. National Archives RG 92, P&R, #139)

Below: Plan of Fort Brady. The entrance of the ship canal to Lake Superior lies beyond the top left corner of the plan. (U.S. National Archives RC 92, Blueprint File, Fort Brady #1)

1890

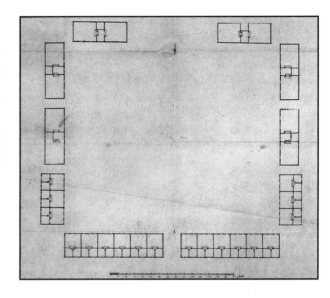

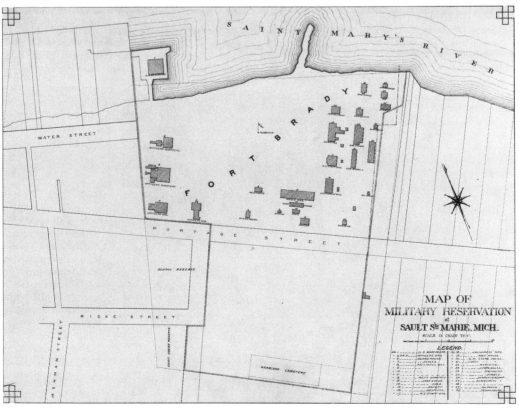

FORT WAYNE

c . 1889

Above: The outer post at Fort Wayne, as seen from the walls of the fortifications. At the extreme right is the "bridge," a ramp built to provide easy acces to the fortifications from the open post. The large brick building in the more distant right is the post hospital, built in 1889 as one of the first new structures in the general conversion from wooden to brick buildings. The Detroit River runs parallel to the direction of this view, and is off camera at the extreme left. (U.S. National Archives 92-F-77-2)

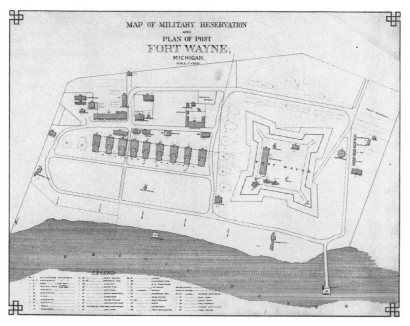

Left: Map of Fort Wayne Military Reservation. The actual fort is to the right; it has overflowed into an extensive military post outside the walls. This is the period when the word "Fort" began to be extended to unfortified military posts. (U.S. National Archives RG 92, Blueprint File, Fort Wayne #1)

c . 1887

FORT WAYNE

1868

Right: This "Sketch of Detroit River" shows the distance in those horse-drawn days between the City of Detroit and Fort Wayne. The river was the fastest route, but it might be controlled by Canada. (U.S. National Archives RG 77, Fort File, Dr. 137-3)

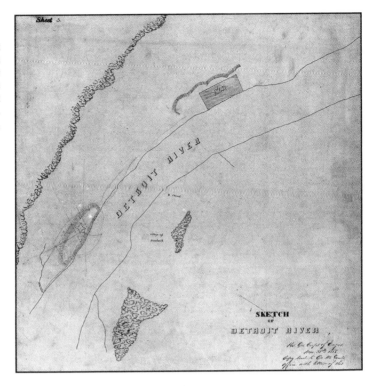

FORT HOLMES/FORT MACKINAC
1843

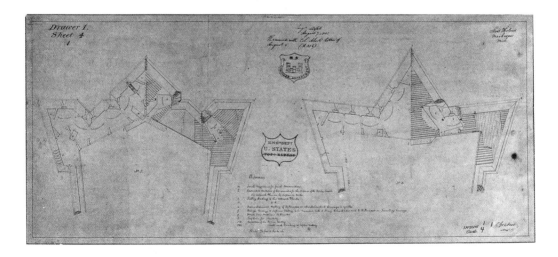

Above: Fort Holmes, the blockhouse and simple earthwork guarding the height of land behind Fort Mackinac, had unaccountably deteriorated into ruins and had almost disappeared. In that year a new two-level redoubt was proposed as an improved Fort Holmes, but it was never built. These plans show that proposal. (U.S. National Archives RG 77, Fort File, Fr. 1-4-1)

5
AFTER 1814

Changing international conditions gradually made fortifications on the Great Lakes seem less necessary, and improved artillery, developed just in time for the Civil War, could destroy masonry walls from a distance and thus made most forts obsolete. The forts often were too cramped for more recent needs, and so military posts simply overflowed the walls of several forts and became small towns, frequently occupying more land than the forts themselves. At Fort Wayne, the construction of a post outside the small fort itself may have begun before the establishment was finally garrisoned in 1861 to handle mobilization for the Civil War. The officers' lines at Fort Wayne, Michigan, in 1869 are much like streets in many middle-class neighborhoods of the day–even including the mud. (U.S. War Department General Staff photo, U.S. National Archives 165-FF-5E-2)

After the War of 1812, the boundary between Canada and the United States was put back essentially where it had been before the war. An international commission was set up to determine exactly where the boundary lay; in the more remote areas its location had never been definitely fixed on the ground.

Soldiers of each country moved back to forts in their own territory; the United States withdrew from Forts Erie and Malden and re-occupied Forts Niagara and Mackinac. Each country also rebuilt and expanded its military posts. The United States rebuilt Fort Dearborn at Chicago and established such new posts as Fort Brady at Sault Ste. Marie and Fort Howard (present-day Green Bay, Wisconsin). Britain continued to improve Fort York and turned Fort Henry into a highly developed nineteenth-century citadel.

The newly drawn boundary line caused some problems. The British garrison at Mackinac withdrew in 1815 to Drummonds Island, which would surely be on the Canadian side of the boundary, and built a post there—only to find in 1822 that the boundary survey gave the island to the United States. As a result, in 1828 the garrison moved again to Penetanguishene, safely in Canadian territory at the foot of Georgian Bay, where there already was a small naval base.

Also after the War of 1812, the dispute between the two British fur-trade companies flared brutally.

The North West Company partners watched in growing alarm as Lord Selkirk, the Scot who now controlled the Hudson's Bay Company, brought in settlers in 1812 and 1814 and established them in the Red River area. Not only was that area central to the fur trade, but it was also the place from which native hunters went out to shoot buffalo from which they made the pemmican that was the staple food of voyageurs who worked for either of the fur trading companies. In the spring of 1814 the governor of Selkirk's Red River Settlement, Miles Macdonell, forbad the export of pemmican from the region, thus shutting off the Northwesters' supply.

During the annual meeting that summer at Fort William, their field headquarters, the anger of the North West partners was extreme. The embargo on pemmican was a serious blow to their trade. Something had to be done. And so a warrant was issued by one of the partners who was a Canadian justice of the peace; according to law, criminal acts taking place in the British Indian Territories could be tried in Canada proper, which at that time lay far to the east. Macdonell was accused of illegally diverting pemmican that belonged to the North West Company, and some of the Northwesters took the warrant back to Red River. They did not serve it at first, but began a campaign of terror and vandalism, destroying crops, burning buildings, and firing mysterious shots in the night. The settlers were forced to retreat northward to Lake Winnipeg while Macdonell, in order to avoid greater violence, agreed to go east via Fort William for trial.

In 1815, however, another party of settlers under a new governor arrived on Hudson Bay and moved southward; and at the same time the Hudson's Bay Company stepped up its competition in the fur trade, organizing a brigade of voyageurs in Montreal to carry the trade into the farthest areas that had formerly been North West Company monopolies. The voyageurs, under Colin Robertson, even came by canoe over the old trade route, carrying HBC goods right past Fort William. Once in the Red River area, Robertson helped the Scots settlers pull themselves together and return to their abandoned farms.

Robertson also seized the northbound express canoe of the North West Company, cap-

Thomas Douglas, Earl of Selkirk, who bought a controlling interest in the Hudson's Bay Company and then precipitated a bloody struggle by attempting to set up a farming community in the middle of the fur country. (Hudson's Bay Company Archives)

turing all of its mail. It was an unprecedented move that made the Northwesters boil with anger, but in the letters he found plans to gather a group of Indians in order to attack the settlement. At this same time Selkirk, who had been in Montreal, came up the Great Lakes with a force of a hundred Swiss mercenaries, men who had come to Canada during the War of 1812 as part of the deMeuron Regiment and had been discharged there.

Meanwhile in the fur country the HBC settlers arrested one of the North West partners and some HBC men burned a North West trading post. Then in mid-July a mounted party of *metis*—men of mixed French and Indian blood— dressed to look like Indians, descended on the settlement. There was a confrontation in which thirty Scots settlers on foot faced the horsemen. Shooting began, during which most of the settlers were killed or wounded, after which the *metis* closed in with knives and guns to kill or mutilate the wounded men. This Massacre of Seven Oaks, as it was called, sent the remaining settlers once again fleeing north toward Lake Winnipeg. Several North West partners, who had waited offstage until the bloody work was done, arrived at that opportune moment to take charge of the area.

Selkirk was at Sault Ste. Marie with his soldiers when he heard of the massacre. He quickly pushed on to Fort William. He camped near the fort and then, accompanied by his men, entered it. There was a struggle between the Swiss and the voyageurs in which no one was really hurt, and then Selkirk held the fort. He had had himself appointed a justice of the peace while he was in Canada, and he now arrested the key Northwesters whom he found in the fort. He also found written evidence that the North West Company had planned the Massacre of Seven Oaks and he found furs that had been stolen from the HBC. Then he sent the Northwesters back east to Canada under guard for trial.

In order to feed his men he bought supplies from the North West partner remaining at Fort William—a man who was not in good standing with the other partners. Then he dispatched Miles Macdonell in charge of some of the soldiers to the Red River area, where Macdonell took control without firing a shot. But perhaps because Selkirk was so convinced of the righteousness of his own cause, he was completely unprepared when a canoe arrived from Canada with a constable bearing a warrant sworn out by the Northwesters for his arrest. Selkirk, whose truly lordly attitude at times compounded his problems, refused to submit— and as soon as the word reached Canada, the North West Company saw that the information got to the highest places. In London, the Colonial Office directed the Canadian government to bring Lord Selkirk to justice forthwith. After wintering at Fort William, Selkirk went on in the spring of 1817 to visit his settlement, then returned through the United States that autumn to face the legal struggle in Canada.

Selkirk spent the rest of his fortune and life (he died in 1820) in Canadian courts, fighting the Northwesters, who knew every legal and political lever to pull against him. He was charged with a multitude of crimes, ranging from larceny of the provisions he bought at Fort William to false arrest. In return, he charged the members of the North West Company with an even vaster array of crimes, including murder. Meanwhile the two companies battled in the fur country until, in 1821, under both government and economic pressure they were forced to combine. The Red River Settlement struggled on with slight agricultural success, but with the protection now of the new combination which bore the old name of Hudson's Bay Company. Trade goods now came in and furs went out mainly through Hudson Bay; Fort William was no longer of key importance, though it continued in existence as an HBC post for another sixty years.

The fur trade in American territory, in the meanwhile, was reserved entirely to U.S. citizens by a bill passed in Congress on April 29, 1816. John Jacob Astor promptly dispatched to Mackinac Island the canny Scot who was to become his right-hand man, Ramsey Crooks. By that July Crooks was at Mackinac, supervising the final year's trading of the South West Company, Astor's partnership with the Montreal traders, and laying the groundwork for Astor's future business. One party sent out by Crooks arrived at Fond du Lac—present-day Duluth—and set out from there for different posts on the upper Mississippi. But men dispatched by Lord Selkirk intercepted them at various points and took them by force to Fort William. In vain they protested that they were on American territory and were working for the South West Company, *not* the North West Company. Selkirk saw little difference. He confiscated their goods and sent them off to Montreal for trial

American Fur Cº⁵ buildings, Fond du Lac. *(Back view.)*

on vague charges. Two of them escaped at Sault Ste. Marie and soon returned to Fond du Lac; there and on their upper Mississippi posts they found that Hudson's Bay traders had been installed in their places.

This, however, was a passing episode. By March of 1817 Astor had bought out his Canadian partners and his American Fur Company had taken over their assets and equipment. The thirty-year-old Ramsey Crooks became its field commander. By 1819 the American fur company was successful enough to hire the first steamer on the upper Lakes, the *Walk-in-the-Water*, to carry a thousand packs of goods to Mackinac Island. Aboard her, in addition to Crooks, came Major General Jacob Brown, now in command of the Northern Department of the U.S. Army, on an inspection tour, and Governor Cass of Michigan Territory. The steamer arrived at Mackinac on June 19, no doubt to the accompaniment of cannon salutes fired from the fort and guards of honor marching from the garrison.

From this time forward, the military posts in the West would have mainly a constabulary function, keeping order in the far-flung wilderness. A typical one was Fort Wilkins, named after Secretary of War William Wilkins, who established it in 1844 at Copper Harbor, Michigan, on the tip of the Keweenaw Peninsula which juts out into Lake Superior. The Chippewa Indians who had held title to the land between present-day

American Fur Company post, Fond du Lac (present-day Duluth). In 1816, when traders of the American Fur Company set out from fond du Lac to posts on the upper Mississippi, men sent by Lord Selkirk intercepted them and took them back by force to Fort William, where Selkirk confiscated their goods and sent them on to Montreal for trial on vague charges., Two who escaped and went back to their posts found Hudson's Bay traders installed in their places at Fond du Lac and the Mississippi posts. But by 1827, the time of this picture, the American Fur Company was firmly in charge in its own territory. (Library of Congress)

Marquette, Michigan, and Duluth, Minnesota, under pressure from mining interests ceded it to the U.S. government in 1842. One band of Chippewas, however, refused to leave their holdings on Isle Royale. The boom town of Copper Harbor, which had sprung up as soon as the territory was opened, now feared Indian reprisals, and the two-company infantry post was the government's answer. Whether because of the fort or not, Indian hostilities never developed. The soldiers were withdrawn in 1846 for service in the Mexican War and the post remained on caretaker status or was used for other purposes until 1867, when it was regarrisoned. In 1870 Fort Wilkins was finally closed.

Those posts farther east, however, had more usual military responsibilities during the lengthy period of cold war between the United States and Canada that followed the War of 1812. The strongest of the Great Lakes forts was Fort Henry at Kingston. Developed to protect the British naval base at Kingston and the upper end of the Rideau Canal (which had been built to connect Lake Ontario with the Ottawa River and thus remove the Canadian line of communications from the St. Lawrence, which was exposed to American attack), it was the second strongest fortification in all of Canada, next only to the citadel at Quebec.

And there were border problems between the two countries. In 1837 the editor-politician William Lyon Mackenzie staged a revolt in Toronto with a handful of armed supporters and was quickly beaten. Mackenzie fled to the United States and attempted to raise an army with which to invade Canada. The whole thing had a comic-opera flavor, except that people got killed.

President Van Buren gave General Winfield Scott the impossible job of single-handedly discouraging attacks on Canada

Fort Wilkins was built in 1844 on Lake Superior at the town of Copper Harbor, Michigan, to protect the booming copper country from Indians. A typical stockaded frontier fort, it was placed on caretaker status during the Mexican War, then regarrisoned until the soldiers left in 1870. After that it may again have been on caretaker status, for in this 1892 photo the buildings are still in reasonably good condition. If the protective stockade remains, it is behind the foliage. The picture looks across the small inland Lake Fanny Hooe. Lake Superior is in the background; note the Copper Harbor Lighthouse in the right distance. (Marquette County Historical Society)

without using any force. Scott in his Memoirs concisely described the situation:

> *In the winter of 1837-'8, a singular disturbance broke out on the lake and northern frontiers of the Union. A number of radicals, in the Canadas, had, a little earlier, begun to agitate in favor of certain revolutionary changes, with an eye on the part of many, toward ultimate annexation to the United States. The heat of the strife soon crossed the frontiers and extended, in many directions, to the depth of forty and sixty miles into the United States. More than two hundred thousand Americans took the infection, organized themselves into lodges, bound by oath to secrecy, and ridiculously enough, without ever having been in Canada, called themselves* **Canadian Patriots!** *—eager to invade the province and fight for* **their** *rights !!*

In 1838 a Mackenzie "army" of several hundred American adventurers, led by a thirty-one-year-old Polish immigrant and former major in the Polish army, Nils Von Schoultz—Mackenzie himself stayed well away from the fighting—invaded Canada at Prescott, on the upper St. Lawrence. The local American authorities carefully looked the other way while the invasion was launched from upstate New York. The Cana-

Construction of a new Fort Henry on the site of the older one at Kingston began in 1832 and was largely completed by 1836. It was then much the strongest fort on the Great Lakes. Here it is in 1839. The gallows for Nils von Schoultz, who led an American invasion of Canada, is just to the left of the fort. Watercolor by H.F. Ainslie. (National Archives of Canada C510)

dians parried the attack in a battle during which twenty of the Americans and eighteen of the defenders were killed. They captured most of the invaders including their leader, imprisoning them in Fort Henry, and the key members were tried in the fort by a Militia Court Martial—that is, a court of Canadian officers, not British regulars. Von Schoultz, who had romantically imagined he was freeing Canadians from oppression, freely pled guilty to leading the invasion. He aroused some sympathy from the Canadian court, which directed that despite his plea, all the evidence be brought before it for consideration; inevitably he was found guilty; but instead of being hanged publicly as were some of the other key invaders, he was hanged on a special gallows built just outside the walls. A few of the less-important leaders were transported to the penal colony in Van Dieman's Land (present-day Tasmania), off the coast of Australia. The young boys were pardoned and sent home.

Meanwhile, farther west in Ohio, plans had been made for an invasion of Canada from Detroit. In September 1838, at a joint convention in Cleveland of American "Hunting Lodges"— the loosely affiliated anti-British secret societies located along the U.S. northern border—an Akron attorney, Louis V. Bierce, was made commander-in-chief of the "Army of the Northwest." On December 4 he led two hundred men through the streets of Detroit, demanding "vengeance" on Canada; they seized a steamer lying at the dock (apparently by collusion with her owner) and crossed the Detroit River to Windsor, where they set fire to a Canadian steamer. They came upon an unarmed British army surgeon and killed him with an axe, but then met a Canadian militia company and fired a few shots at it. One well-aimed Canadian volley sent the invaders running, leaving behind their dead and wounded. The steamer that brought them to Canada had long since departed to safer waters, so they stole whatever boats and canoes they could find, rushing back to the American shore.

At Oswego, which had been a staging point for Von Schoultz's invasion, and at Detroit and in northern Ohio, anti-Canadian feeling ran high. The United States government took an ambivalent attitude: it knew that local politicians supported the invaders, but it found the invasions to be diplomatically embarrassing. Oddly enough, these opposing feelings seem to have led to the construction of two new forts. One was a third Fort Ontario at Oswego, the other was Fort Wayne, nearDetroit on the river front. On the one hand the forts would control the coastline and prevent further expeditions being organized there,

while on the other they were gestures of defiance toward the Britons across the border. Fort Ontario, located in an area where feelings were near the boiling point because of the capture and punishment of invaders who came from that region, was built in 1839-44; Fort Wayne, located where enthusiasm had been somewhat cooled by the invaders' panic-stricken retreat—and where there already were soldiers in barracks—was not completed until 1851 and not manned until 1861.

Members of the Confederate army and navy based in Canada launched an abortive attack against the United States across Lake Erie in 1864, and following the Civil War in 1866 the Fenian Brotherhood, an Irish-American patriotic organization that also seemed to come straight out of *opera bouffe* , except

The third version of Fort Ontario, at Oswego, seen here under construction in the 1840s. (Fort Ontario State Historic Site)

In 1870 at Fort Ontario, Oswego, N.Y., soldiers pose outside their barracks. (U.S. Signal Corps photo, U.S. National Archives 111-SC-88040)

that they were former Union army soldiers carrying loaded guns, invaded Canada from Buffalo with perhaps a thousand men, based themselves in the ruins of abandoned Fort Erie, and for a time marched into Canada and battled Canadian militia.

But generally, the forts had had their day. The British army left Canada in 1870, and Fort Henry slowly deteriorated. The U.S. Army abandoned Fort Mackinac in 1895. American units stayed on at Forts Ontario, Niagara, and Wayne, simply expanding beyond the old fortifications and turning the surrounding land into modern military posts which continued in use until after World War II. Following the Civil War a more convenient Fort Brady was built at Sault Ste. Marie. In 1901 a third Fort Brady, a typical open post of the area, was built there. It too was used until 1944.

The only new military base that appeared on the

Great Lakes was Fort Sheridan. By the mid-1880s Fort Dearborn had long disappeared from Chicago. But since its disappearance, there had been one event in the city that called for use of federal troops on a large scale—the Chicago fire of October 1871, to which were rushed units of the 5th Infantry from Fort Leavenworth, Kansas, to establish martial law, stop looting, and restore order. General Phil Sheridan was in command. Then in 1886 the Haymarket Riot led civic leaders to wish that a permanent military force was stationed comfortably nearby. The Commercial Club of Chicago offered land for an army post to the government, and in

The second Fort Brady at Sault Ste. Marie, seen here probably in the 1880s, is a typical unfortified military post. (Chippewa County Historical Society)

November 1887 the first units arrived at what, the following year, was officially named Fort Sheridan.

But it was not a true fort, simply a military post in a flat, open area along the shore of Lake Michigan. There would be no more forts.

At Fort Niagara in 1879 the "French Castle" is recognizable, even with its Victorian embellishments. The pedestal for a navigational light, placed there some time after the War of 1812, remains at center, though the light itself has been moved elsewhere (U.S. Signal Corps photo, U.S. National Archives 111-SC-88035)

LIFE IN THE FORTS

Above: Living room of the Fort Mackinac quarters to which Lieutenant Morse brought his bride in 1890. Picture taken in March of that year. These quarters were in the oldest stone building, which dates from the British construction of the fort. (Courtesy of the late B.C. Morse, Jr.)

Left: At Fort Mackinac, a picture taken between 1884 and 1890 shows Lt. Benjamin Clarke Morse (later a World War I general) with his company of the 23rd Infantry, in front of the barracks built in 1859. (Courtesy the late B.C. Morse, Jr.)

Right: At Fort Brady c.1880, a field battery of 32-pounders still is pointed across the river to Canada. (Chippewa County Historical Society)

MILITARY LIFE
SOLDIERS: YESTERDAY ...

Above: At New Fort Brady (the third military post of that name at Sault Ste. Marie) in the early 1900s, a unit stands inspection. Note the change in uniform from that worn after the Civil War. The barracks building in the background is typical of U.S. Army construction of the period. (Lake Superior State University)

Above: The garrison of Fort York, at Toronto, needed more liveable peacetime quarters and in 1841 overflowed into a "New Fort" built nearby. The new post was essentially a set of stone buildings unfortified except for a surrounding palisade. In 1870, the British army withdrew from Canada and turned the fort over to the Canadian army. Here in 1887 Canadian soldiers relax in the canteen of "New Fort York." (National Archives of Canada C31462)

... AND SOLDIERS TODAY

Above: Inside Fort Meigs, the modern reconstruction of a stockaded camp near present-day Toledo, Ohio, built by William Henry Harrison during the winter of 1812-13. The piled-up earth at right is the end of one of the traverses, earthen walls across the inside of the fort that stopped the rolling and bouncing cannon balls thrown into it by British cannon. (Photo by author)

Right: A drummer and fifer demonstrate their instruments at Fort York. (Photo by author)

Below: On the parade ground at Fort Niagara, a demonstration of 1812 tactics. (Photo by author)

Above: The Fort Henry guard demonstrating its drill. (Parks of the St. Lawrence)

Below: At Fort Henry, a soldier of the Royal Artillery–played by a member of the Fort Henry Guard–prepares one of the large cannon on the walls. (Parks of the St. Lawrence)

CIVILIAN LIFE IN THE FORTS

Left: A blacksmith at work in the artificers' building at Fort George. (Fort George)

Right: An interpreter plays the part of a washerwoman at Fort Wilkins. (Michigan History Division)

6

THE SENTINELS THAT REMAIN

Many of the forts still exist or have been restored. Most are open to the public during the summer months; some are open on a limited basis year-around. Visitors can see tangible structures illustrating the history of the region and can feel something of the life in those days and places.

Left: Fort Mackinac looks down from its island hilltop. The park at the foot of the hill was once the vegetable garden for the fort. A statue of the pioneer missionary, Father Marquette, stands in the park. (Mackinac State Historic Parks)

FORT BRADY

Sault Ste. Marie, joining Lakes Huron and Superior, has been a strategic location throughout history. (In World War II, antiaircraft defenses were placed here.) French forts were built at the Sault, British military forts were built nearby on St. Joseph and Drummond Islands, and a fort of the British trading companies stood on the Canadian shore. On the American side, the U.S. Army built Fort Brady—or rather, three Fort Bradys.

The first of these forts, a palisaded frontier post built in 1822 by Colonel (later General) Hugh Brady to counter the British garrison at Drummond Island, has long disappeared, although some archaeological work has been done on it. The second, a post-Civil-War open station (but with guns in position facing Canada) was built on the same site in the late 1860s during a period of strong anti-British feeling in the U.S. Fragments of it still exist in the form of houses that now are in private hands.

The third Fort Brady—still known today as "New Fort Brady"—was constructed a short distance away from that site, with work beginning in the 1890s and lasting through the turn of the century. It continued as an active military post, without any fortifications, until 1944. It now houses Lake Superior State University, where a visitor can see a number of military buildings dating from 1901 to 1940.

Above: Post Headquarters, New Fort Brady, now the university counseling center. (Photo by Robert Money)

Below: Officers' row, New Fort Brady, now university offices and dormitories. (Photo by Robert Money)

Above: Post Guard House, New Fort Brady. The building is now occupied by Lake Superior State University (Photo by Robert Money)

Below: Officers' quarters of the second Fort Brady are now used as a private home. (Photo by Robert Money)

FORT ERIE

Fort Erie stands where Lake Erie funnels into the Niagara River. Directly across the river from Buffalo, N.Y., it is in what now is the city of Fort Erie, Ontario, today best known for its racetrack. The first British fort here—and the first all-British fort built on the Great Lakes—was constructed on the site of a French trading post in 1764 and was destroyed by storm-driven ice 15 years later. Rebuilt a short distance southward, the palisaded fort was again destroyed by ice in 1803. The third fort, made of stone, was built farther from the water in 1807. Initially it was the Lake Erie terminus of the portage from Lake Ontario to Lake Erie, around Niagara Falls. (Fort Niagara was at the Lake Ontario end.)

Although the stone fort was not completed by the beginning of the 1812 War, American forces that attacked on November 28 from Black Rock, near Buffalo, were driven back. In May of 1813, after British regular units had been withdrawn and the fort was defended only by local militia, U.S. forces took it, but in early June they abandoned it. The British reoccupied it in December of 1813. Early the following July a heavy U.S. attack swallowed it up.

After the major Battle of Lundy's Lane, American forces fell back on the fort and began to build up its defenses. For five months in 1814 it was occupied by U.S. forces and through much of that time was besieged by the British. (A reminder of that bloody siege, with its attacks and counterattacks, was the military cemetery discovered in 1987 on private property near the fort.) The British raised the unsuccessful siege in September, and in early November the Americans destroyed as much of the fort as possible, pulling back across the Niagara River to U.S. territory.

The fort was repaired and reoccupied, but then abandoned by the British in 1823. Its

Inside Fort Erie. (Photo by the author)

ruins were used as a base by the Fenian Brotherhood when that Irish-American group invaded Canada from Buffalo following the U.S. Civil War. Restoration of the fort began in 1934 as a Great Depression work project, though during World War II the fort deteriorated. In 1949 restoration began again. Today the fort stands as it was in August 1814, when it was held by Americans and besieged by the British in the only true siege in any theater of the entire war.

Erie is a four-sided earth and masonry fort with a ravelin (a V-shaped outerwork pointing away from the fort) to protect the gate and the inner stone walls on the water side. On the land side what at first look like bastions (diamond-shaped structures that protrude from the corners of a fort) are actually redoubts (detached stone defences tied to the main fort only by earthworks). The redoubts would no doubt have become bastions of the fort if extended masonry walls could have been built, but at no time during the war was either side able to make the fort a complete defensive structure. The original, incomplete British works were mated with hasty American additions.

Within the fort a visitor can see the guardroom, barracks, kitchen, and officers' quarters. Costumed staff members play the parts of the women who baked bread in the kitchen of the officers' quarters and of the soldiers who drilled on the parade ground. Each year there are re-enactments of the 1814 fighting. A series of educational programs, covering subjects ranging from a general history of the area to archaeological work, are available for visiting groups of students. An overnight program brings students into the routine of the former garrison. The visitor, by firmly shutting out what lies beyond the walls, can be carried back 150 years.

Right: Fort Erie, site of a bloody seige during the War of 1812. The fort was not completed before the war, and the two redoubts in the foreground were never linked by stone walls to the rest of the fort. (Travelpic Publications, Niagara Falls)

Below: Inside the reconstructed fort, stone barracks at left, earthworks at right. (Photo by the author)

FORT GEORGE

Fort George, built mainly of wood and earthworks, is on the Niagara River at the picturesque town of Niagara-on-the-Lake, Ontario. After the British turned over Fort Niagara to the new United States in 1796, they built this fort to guard their side of the river. The site of the fort was originally a storage and administrative installation which was not ideally placed as a fortification; when Fort George was completed in 1802 its guns did not command the river mouth and its long, relatively thin shape made it hard to defend.

During the War of 1812, the original fort was battered by the American guns of Fort Niagara, partly rebuilt by the Americans when they captured it, largely destroyed by the Americans when they retreated from it, and partly rebuilt again by the British after they retook it. In 1812-13 the British, rebuilding the fort, changed it from the previous shape to a more compact and defensible form. Thus it changed considerably during the latter part of its history.

Toward the end of the war the British also built, on the flank of Fort George, the fortified coastal defence battery of Fort Mississauga, more directly across the river from Fort Niagara. Soon after the war the garrison of Fort George was moved to Fort York; George deteriorated and the small Fort Mississauga (a star fort—one without bastions—which from the air resembles a conventionalized star) became the main base in the area. Its surrounding grounds were used for training camps through World War I. Now the remains of Mississauga, which seem tiny, lie in the middle of a golf course and must be viewed from a distance by all except the golfers. Fort George was reconstructed in 1937-40 from the British plans of the time before the Americans captured it, and is open to the public.

Fort George today forms its original stretched-out hexagon, two long walls facing the Niagara River and two facing inland, with a short wall at either end. There are bastions at each corner of the walls, the one facing the river at the central corner being larger than the others and housing the main battery of the fort. The single original building that remains is the stone powder magazine. During the Battle of Queenston Heights, on October 13, 1812, an American red-hot cannonball went through the roof of the magazine and set fire to the wooden supports of the roof. With 800 barrels of gunpowder in the magazine, the situation was dangerous enough that the fort was temporarily evacuated. A small group of soldiers led by Captain Vigoreux of the Royal Engineers climbed onto the magazine roof, tore away the metal roofing, and put out the fire.

The reconstructed buildings include blockhouse barracks, officers' quarters and kitchen, guardhouse, and an artificer's building in which costumed interpreters play the parts of the men who maintained the weapons and the fort, working with iron and wood. Other interpreters, in British uniforms of 1812, portray the soldiers who were stationed here.

Below: The small Fort Mississauga, built as an artillery emplacement to guard the northern flank of Fort George. The original tower—made of brick salvaged from the nearby town after it was burned by American forces during the War of 1812—stands inside the original earthworks. Today the fort is surrounded by a golf course. (Photo by author)

Above: In the reconstructed Fort George, the stone powder magazine is the only original building remaining. (Photo by author)

Below: Fort George as seen from the air. (Fort George)

Previous Page Bottom: The interior of Fort George. (Photo by author)

GRAND PORTAGE

Grand Portage—the Great Carrying Place—was the trail over which canoes and trade goods were taken from the head of Lake Superior to Pigeon River and thence proceeded to the interior. When the British took control from the French they too used the carrying place, and traders began to erect posts at the Lake Superior end of it. That location became known by the same name as the trail.

As traders went ever farther north and west, Grand Portage became the place where canoe brigades from Montreal met those from the interior each July at the annual rendezvous to exchange trade goods for furs, and where at the same time the traders held yearly business meetings, punctuated by feasting and dancing. By 1778 the group of traders that was to become the North West Company had established a sizable fort here, "picketed in with cedar palisadoes," according to Alexander Mackenzie, the explorer who was first to cross the continent north of Mexico. Soon the company fort had sixteen buildings inside the palisade, and development of the establishment went on almost until its abandonment in 1803, when the company moved its base to Fort William.

The fort at Grand Portage was taken over briefly by a rival group, the XY Company, that had had a smaller post nearby. But when in 1804 the XY Company amalgamated with the Nor'Westers and joined them at Fort William, the Grand Portage fort quickly deteriorated. By the 1820s, travellers saw only some depressions in the ground where buildings had once stood.

Today in Grand Portage National Monument, just on the United States side of the international boundary, the fort stands on its original site, a high palisade again surrounding it. The Great Hall has been rebuilt and now contains numerous displays. Each August the National Monument and the Grand Portage Band of the Chippewa Tribe host a re-creation of Rendezvous Days, with voyageur and Indian activities and demonstrations. The portage trail is open year around. It still covers 8 1/4 miles of wild country, and experienced hikers can cross it as the voyageurs once did—but without carrying the voyageurs' heavy loads of furs and supplies.

Above: Grand Portage, the fort at the Lake Superior end of the portage, has been partly rebuilt on the site of the fur-trade fort. The reconstructed Great Hall at Grand Portage is seen here. (Grand Portage National Monument)

Right: A modern interpreter at Grand Portage demonstrates the load that was normally carried by a voyageur over the 8 1/4 mile-long portage. Present-day hikers can cross the portage with less cargo. (Grand Portage National Monument)

FORT HENRY

Fort Henry at Kingston, Ontario is the strongest fort ever built on the Great Lakes. After the War of 1812 the British decided to build a new citadel to protect Kingston, the linkpin between Lower Canada (now Quebec) and Upper Canada (Ontario). The Duke of Wellington, analyzing the lessons of the war and studying the geography of North America, decided that "there must be a good fort at Point Henry."

The fort built during the war was torn down and the new one begun in 1832 and completed in 1848. The regiments stationed there until the British army left Canada in 1870 had resounding names—among them the Royal Welch Fusiliers, the Black Watch, The Highland Light Infantry, the Duke of Wellington's Regiment, and the Royal Regiment of Artillery.

The fort is six-sided, its walls straight lines with no bastions. It has an advanced battery (the long, pointed extension commanding the harbor). Within five of the walls are casemates (galleries built into the walls) that provide space for all the functions of the fort, from guardhouse to barracks, that otherwise would require buildings. The fort proper is surrounded by a dry ditch—a moat without water; cannon or musket fire could sweep the ditch, clearing away any attack near the walls and supplanting the bastions found on most earlier forts. Two other deep, stone-faced ditches that run down the east and west slopes below the fort are covered by wall-mounted cannon, aimed to fire straight along them, thus drastically hindering any attempt to maneuver troops around the fort. Cannon are mounted on all the walls except the one directly behind the forward battery, which of course mounts its own cannon.

After 1870, the Canadian army soon abandoned the fort except for a caretaker. Slowly it deteriorated, though during World War I it was a prisoner-of-war camp. A hundred years after it first was built, the Canadian and Ontario governments during the Great Depression put nearly a thousand men to work in a major project that completely restored Fort Henry. During World War II it was both a prisoner-of-war camp and an internment camp for civilians of enemy nations who were found in Canada.

Old Fort Henry was one of the first military museums anywhere to use live interpretation, forming the Fort Henry Guard in 1938. The Guard, made up largely of college students, wears the uniforms, carries the weapons, and follows the drill of the British army of the 1860s. Its members guide visitors around the fort, but it is best known as a highly trained drill team, having performed at the Royal Tournament in London and in joint ceremonies with the United States Marine Corps both at the fort and in Washington.

Visitor tours of the fort are conducted in English, French, or German. Special events available for children range from a "Children's Military Muster" through activities in a Victorian schoolroom, to a Punch-and-Judy puppet show.

The day at the fort begins with a flag raising, is punctuated with gun salutes, drills, and daily parades, and ends with the flag lowering. As did British regiments of the period that it represents, the Guard has an animal mascot—a highly groomed goat—and each day there is a "Goat Mascot Walkabout." Each week there are sunset formations and tattoos; visiting organizations such as highland pipe bands often perform. National holidays usually are celebrated at the fort with particular ceremony.

Right: Fort Henry Guard uses the uniforms and drill of the British army of the 1860s. (Parks of the St. Lawrence)

Below: Fort Henry, on Point Henry at Kingston, Ontario. Fort Henry, the most powerful fort on the Great Lakes, was largely completed by 1836, with smaller additions made during the 1840s. Barracks, mess hall, and other administrative activities of the fort are located in case-mates within the walls. Large forts built at this time began to depart from the older pattern and often had no bastions, close-in defense being provided in other ways, here mainly by the dry ditch or moat, which could be swept by fire. The advanced battery—the long extension—controlled the harbor and its imme-diate surroundings. (Parks of the St. Lawrence)

FORT HOWARD

At Green Bay, the oldest settlement in Wisconsin, the 40-acre Heritage Hill State Park contains a number of old and reconstructed buildings that show the history of the region. In the park, a military heritage area has several buildings from Fort Howard—a company mess, a hospital, and officers' quarters among them. During the summer there are military re-enactments here.

Fort Howard was built in 1816 on the site of earlier French and British forts. Most of the civilians already settled in the area were of French descent. The United States needed to project its power into this distant part of its territory, and was encouraged by John Jacob Astor, who wanted to be certain that British fur traders based in Canada were blocked from reaching the Indians of the region. The fort was named for a general of the War of 1812. Some of the officers stationed here would go on to distinguished careers; probably the best known was Major Zachary Taylor, here from 1817 to 1820. Among the others was Major William Whistler, father of the noted painter, stationed at Howard in 1827 and 1828.

Construction was that of a typical frontier military post. The first barracks were built of logs and the fort was surrounded by a stockade thirty feet high, with blockhouses at the angles to act as wooden bastions. Then beginning in 1831, the post was rebuilt with frame buildings, which had distinctive French dormer windows similar to those of private homes nearby. As the post grew, it also attracted additional settlers, mainly of people doing business with it in one way or another—everyone from grocers to prostitutes.

Over the years the units stationed at Howard sallied forth on various expeditions against the Indians, including the Black Hawk War, but the fort was never attacked. Red Bird, a Winnebago chief who led a rebellion against the encroaching United States, was imprisoned and eventually died here. Detachments from the fort also acted as federal police, enforcing U.S. laws against squatting on federal lands or peddling whiskey to the Indians; whether during military or police activity, the fort achieved its purpose of showing the American flag on the frontier.

In 1841 all troops were withdrawn to participate in the Seminole Wars in Florida. The fort was regarrisoned in 1849, then again put on caretaker status in 1852. It came to life once more as a mobilization center during the Civil War, but in 1863 the War Department turned it over to the Department of the Interior Land Office, for sale as civilian land. In 1869 its buildings were torn down or taken away.

Fort Howard officers' quarters, a reconstruction built at Heritage Hill, Green Bay. (Heritage Hill)

Above: An original building, a detached kitchen, used to prepare meals for the Fort Howard garrison. It was moved to Heritage Hill in 1975, and is used by interpreters to show many aspects of life at the fort. Other buildings, like the Fort Howard Hospital, are currently being restored. The Hospital was built in 1834 and after the fort closed was located in several places around Green Bay, since 1929 as a museum. In 1975 it was moved to Heritage Hill where it is used to display and explain medical techniques of the Fort Howard era. (Heritage Hill)

Right: Interior of the Fort Howard Hospital undergoing restoration at Heritage Hill, Green Bay. (Heritage Hill)

FORT MACKINAC

Fort Mackinac, the island fort in the straits, was occupied by soldiers until 1895 and then was turned over to the State of Michigan for use as a park. The fort became the center of a recreational area and as a result was not greatly changed over the years. While it was not too well maintained, neither was it permitted to fall apart as tourists wandered over it.

In the 1950s, growing public interest in history led to the excavation and reconstruction of Fort Michilimackinac on the nearby mainland. As the project went forward, interest also grew in the history of Fort Mackinac and there followed a general restoration of it to show how this fort was in the days when soldiers were stationed here.

The fort was built initially by the British and first manned by them in 1781, but after the American Revolution and the Treaty of Ghent, it was turned over to the U.S. Army in 1796. Roughly triangular in shape, with masonry walls overlooking the high limestone bluffs that face the water, with a blockhouse at the point of the triangle and others at the centers of the two arms facing inland, Fort Mackinac, plus its outlying blockhouse Fort Holmes, was a hard nut to crack by any nineteenth-century attack that could be mounted against this isolated position. A long ramp that leads up to the fort from shore level ends at the south sally port. A frontal attack would have been almost impossible. The north sally port leads out through the northern wall onto the hilltop, where there were stables and a rifle range—and land slightly higher than the fort.

The one attack that succeeded came at the beginning of the War of 1812. The government in Washington did not bother to tell the commander of the fort that they had declared war, but the British at nearby Fort St. Joseph were notified promptly. After a quiet landing at the low, northern end of the island, British soldiers made their way south to the high ground behind the fort, and Lt. Porter Hanks, the U. S. commanding officer, suddenly discovered them there with their weapons trained down on him. (As soon as the British gained the fort, they built a protective blockhouse on that high ground, which from then on was maintained by both British and American garrisons. Following the war it was named Fort Holmes, after a young American officer killed in a subsequent—and ineffective— U.S. attempt to recapture the fort.) In 1815, the post was again returned to the Americans, and the British garrison moved to Drummond Island.

Today one can stand on the parade ground in the middle of the refurbished fort, among fourteen of the original buildings within the original walls, and readily imagine how successive generations of British and American soldiers drilled here. Often during the summer there also are nearby encampments of organizations that play such roles as colonial militia or French-and-Indian-War regiments. Guided tours within the fort take the visitor through the points of interest, including the restored quarters of officers and their families, which are shown by costumed interpreters. There is a separate children's walking tour which gives younger people the opportunity to handle artifacts and ask questions.

During the summer, interpreters wearing American uniforms of the 1880s drill and fire rifles on the parade ground, and fire cannon from the bluffs. Uniformed musicians provide fife, drum, and bugle music for the drills, and sometimes add the bag-pipe to their regular concerts each day. Uniformed interpreters demonstrate fire-arms of the types used during the century-plus of the fort's existence. And although it may be impossible for us to feel today the utter isolation of what during the early 1800s was the northernmost military post in the United States, the view of the straits from the gun platform at Inspiration Point seems to have changed little over the years.

Right: At Fort Mackinac, interpreters in the U.S. Army uniform of the late 1800s demonstrate a field gun for visitors. At this time armies of the world emulated the Prussian army, including the spiked helmets. (Mackinac State Historic Parks)

Below: Fort Mackinac as seen from the eastern wall. (Mackinac State Historic Parks)

FORT MALDEN

Fort Malden is at Amherstburg, Ontario, a few miles south of Windsor on the Detroit River. It became important as a British base after Detroit was ceded to the United States—in the person of Anthony Wayne—in 1796. British vessels were repaired or constructed here over the years, and the British squadron that fought Oliver Hazard Perry on Lake Erie in 1813 was made ready for battle and, in part, built here. American forces captured it in September, 1813, following Perry's victory, but in 1815, after the war, it was returned to the British. In 1837-38 it became a center for Canadian defense against the American invaders who styled themselves "Patriots." Throughout its later military history, the fort was roughly square, with spearhead-shaped bastions at each corner. Artillery was mounted on the earthworks. There were about a dozen buildings inside the walls, including two barracks that housed about two hundred soldiers each. It was garrisoned until 1851, then was put on caretaker status until 1859, when it was converted to a lunatic asylum. In 1870 the land was taken over by a lumber company and later, houses were built on parts of it.

Today, in the pleasant Fort Malden National Historic Park, one bit of the earthworks remains. It is the northwest bastion, looking out over the river. There is a one-story brick barracks that was built in 1819-20, then in the 1840s converted to a hospital. Other structures were built after the army left. One, the Hough House, is a handsome building that at first was part of the asylum and in the 1920s became a private residence; today it houses an excellent exhibit of old British uniforms and accouterments, and other historical exhibits. A small orientation building, erected in 1939, stands outside the limits of the original post but inside those of the present-day park and contains a small auditorium plus exhibits that explain the layout and history of the fort. Interpreters present military demonstrations, usually on weekends.

Above: Ford Malden. At left is an original building that was a barracks, then a hospital. At right, the Hough House. (Photo by author)

Right: At Fort Malden, the Hough House, built after the fort was deactivated, and in the forground the remaining earthworks of the northwest bastion. (Photo by author)

FORT MEIGS

Fort Meigs, a palisaded fort constructed by General William Henry Harrison early in 1813—and thriftily dismantled again by the government after it had served its purpose—has been reconstructed on its original site by the Ohio Historical Society. It is on the bluffs of the Maumee River, a few miles upstream from Lake Erie at present-day Perrysburg, Ohio. Once more it looks down the Maumee, a strategic highway of the pioneer era. Once more young men patrol its walls in the U.S. Army uniforms of the War of 1812.

Roughly semicircular in shape with the curved wall facing the river, the fort takes best advantage of its hilltop location; two of the five batteries, one of them the "Grand Battery," point toward the river. The main gate, on the landward side, is protected by one of the seven blockhouses built into the walls.

Inside the fort is an area of nearly ten acres, containing the traverses—earthen walls put up to stop the trundling roundshot thrown into the fort by British cannon— blockhouses, and a few other structures. The soldiers lived in tents on the muddy ground between the traverses; the blockhouses and other buildings were used only for defense and storage. Basically, the place was a fortified camp, named for the then-governor of Ohio, Return J. Meigs, and the orders published there were headed "Camp Meigs." The garrison at various times ranged from under 900 to more than 2,000.

Costumed interpreters explain points of interest to visitors; there are nighttime lantern tours; demonstrations of cannon and musket firing and fife-and-drum concerts enliven the picture. Within some of the blockhouses today are exhibits showing what life was like here, how the fort was restored, and what kinds of weapons and artifacts have been unearthed by archaeological work at the fort.

Below: Fort Meigs, on the bank of the Maumee River above Lake Erie, was built during the War of 1812 and torn down after the war. It has been reconstructed on the site, after extensive archaeological and historical research. The monument in the left distance was erected many years ago to mark the site; the reconstructed fort has since been built around it. (Photo by author)

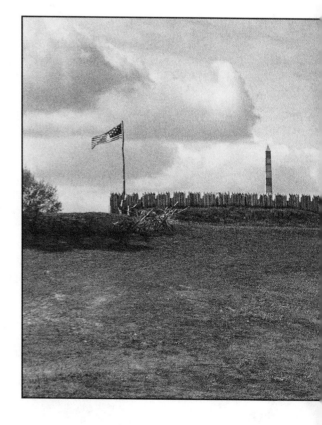

Right: Inside the walls of Fort Meigs. The fort was named for the Ohio governor of the day. (Photo by author)

FORT MICHILIMACKINAC

The wooden, palisaded Fort Michilimackinac has been restored on its original site at what today is Mackinaw City, Michigan, near the southern end of the great Mackinac Bridge that crosses the straits. Built by the French in 1715 and later taken over by the British, the original fort was abandoned when the garrison moved to Mackinac Island in 1781.

Archaeological work began at the site in 1959 to determine just what the old fort was like. That work (which found that the place had gradually been expanded in five stages throughout its history) plus old plans and descriptions became the basis for the present restoration, which shows the fort much as it was during Pontiac's War, when Indians invaded the fort and killed the surprised British garrison there.

Visitors can see how Europeans, at the end of a long and difficult supply route, converted local materials into a fort. Such forts, with palisaded walls and wooden bastions, became the standard means of defense along the frontier. This one, a five-sided enclosure, had a water gate and a land gate, each guarded by an overhanging structure; at each corner of the fort was a bastion from which defenders could direct weapons fire along the outside of the walls.

Visitors can also see how archaeologists discovered much about the fort. An underground archaeological tunnel shows original artifacts as they were found in layers of earth. Ongoing archaeological work can be observed as the digs continue.

Nearby is a Native American encampment, where interpreters in Indian dress demonstrate the life and lore of the area's original inhabitants.

Inside the fort—almost a fortified village—costumed interpreters play the roles of British soldiers, fur traders, voyageurs, and family members. There are a walking tour and a special program for children. The interpreters not only fire muskets and cannon, and demonstrate pioneer skills such as cooking, blacksmithing, and woodworking, but also stage a French Colonial Wedding, the wedding ceremony followed by traditional festivities with music and dancing.

Below: Ste. Anne's Church, reconstructed at Fort Michilimackinac. In the right distance is one of the unusual bastions of the fort—not quite a blockhouse. (Mackinac State Historic.Parks)

Above: Fort Michilimackinac, a reconstruction on the site of the original fort which existed from 1715 to 1781. It is at present-day Mackinaw City; the Mackinac Straits Bridge is in the right distance. (Mackinac State Historic Parks)

Below: Reconstructed barracks at Fort Michilimackinac. The original was built in 1768. (Mackinac State Historic Parks)

FORT NIAGARA

Fort Niagara stands high on the point of land separating the mouth of the Niagara River from Lake Ontario. Of all original forts that remain, Niagara is the oldest. The stone building now known as the "French Castle" was built here in 1726 on the site of earlier, stockaded, French posts, and some of the earthworks were built by Captain Pouchot, last French commander of the fort, in 1755-56.

Stern and gray, the fort overlooks the harbor which today is a haven for sailing yachts as it once was a haven for sailing warships. Within the fort, a visitor will find it spans the centuries with stone redoubts that were built by the British to add strength to the defenses, a furnace built by U.S. engineers in 1839 to heat cannon balls red hot so that they would set fire to enemy ships or forts, and casemates added by the United States during the 1870s. Ongoing archaeological research has shown that at various times over the centuries a total of as many as 250 buildings stood inside the site.

As the fort has evolved, today it forms an irregular shape, very roughly three-sided, with walls above Lake Ontario and the Niagara River, and with particularly heavy earthen walls on the eastern side. These walls follow the line first selected by Captain Pouchot, running between the river and the lake to block off the base of the peninsula where the fort stands. Outside the eastern walls a large V-shaped earthwork called a ravelin points in the direction from which an attack was most likely to come. At the base of the ravelin there originally were two smaller Vs called lunettes, one (which still is there) pointed toward the river and the other (which has disappeared over the years) toward the lake. In the middle of the eastern wall, protected by the ravelin, is the sally port, a tunnel and gate that would permit defenders to sally out and make a counterattack.

On the eastern side there are also two bastions with casemated walls (Casemates are chambers within the walls, in this instance where cannon are mounted so that they can fire defensively through small outer ports. They place the cannon in the most effective positions and protect the gun crews from enemy fire. These casemates were to contain howitzers that would fire anti-personnel loads—grapeshot and canister, which contained many small projectiles, like giant shotgun loads—along the walls. Small arms could also be fired from them.) Completion of the casemates at Fort Niagara, however, came in 1872, after the Civil War had shown that modern cannon could destroy a masonry fort from a distance. By the time they were completed, the casemates were obsolete. In fact, forts such as Niagara were becoming obsolete, and gradually most military activities moved from within the fortifications to "New" Fort Niagara, an open post outside them.

The old fort gradually deteriorated. In 1927 the Old Fort Niagara Association was formed to restore and maintain it; during the 1920s and 30s reconstruction of the timeworn, neglected fortifications began. In a burst of overenthusiasm, the "Gate of the Five Nations" was rebuilt in stone instead of the original wood, but most restoration was more accurate. In 1963 the federal government ceded the property to the State of New York. It in turn converted the area to a state park, razing most of the buildings from the new post outside the walls and licensing the Association to maintain and display the old fortifications.

Today the fort provides frequent displays of military drill in the uniforms of the various periods it was active, and presents other programs to help visitors understand the bloody history of the now-peaceful Niagara region. The fort itself is a solid reminder of times past.

Above: Fort Niagara from the air. The original building, constructed by the French in 1726, is the large structure at extreme left. Lake Ontario is beyond the fort, the mouth of the Niagara River is on the near side. At bottom is a modern U.S. Coast Guard Station. (Old Fort Niagara Assocation)

Below: The Battery Dauphin at Fort Niagara commands the drawbridge of the fort and the former path along the Niagara River. (Old Fort Niagara Assocation)

Fort Niagara once guarded a harbor for sailing warships. Today the sailing vessels carry no cannon. (Photo by author)

FORT ONTARIO

The five-bastioned walls of Fort Ontario were built east of the Oswego River mouth, overlooking Lake Ontario, in 1839-44. They are on the same high bluff at Oswego, N.Y. that has been occupied by a series of British and American forts since 1755. (There were smaller forts in Oswego as early as 1727.)

The best example of classic fort design in the Great Lakes region, Fort Ontario from the air looks much like Fort McHenry, the fort at Baltimore that inspired Francis Scott Key to write *The Star-Spangled Banner*. Its construction was based on precepts set forth by Sebastien de Vauban, the 17th and 18th century Marshal of France and military engineer who was acknowledged as a master of fortifications. Ontario's outline, seen from above, has been compared to a five-pointed star, with diamond-shaped bastions at each point, although technically because it has bastions it is not a star fort. A dry moat surrounded the walls, and outside that were earthworks. Originally the earthworks included a V-shaped demilune pointing inland, in the direction of the most probable attack, but like the moat and other works it has largely disappeared over the years.

This fort was built during a period of Canadian-American tension, after American invaders—self-proclaimed Canadian "Patriots," many of whom had never seen Canada—gathered at Oswego and launched an attack on Canada. The poorly organized and badly supported force was captured by Canadian and British troops, and its leaders hanged. Others were transported to Van Dieman's Land (modern Tasmania), near Australia. The numerous boys who had gone along for the adventure were pardoned and returned to the United States.

Naturally, if not logically, anti-Canadian feeling in the Oswego region boiled even more

During reconstruction of Fort Ontario, massive cannon surround the magazine. (Fort Ontario State Historic Site)

fiercely as a result of the punishments. Naturally at the same time anti-American feeling grew in Canada. The U.S. government, gravely embarrassed diplomatically by the invasion but aware that local politicians supported it enthusiastically, solved two problems by building the fort: it made an apparently defiant anti-Canadian gesture to sooth the populace, yet put federal soldiers where they could block any further invasion moves from Oswego.

During and shortly after the Civil War, the fort was overhauled to bring it up to then-current standards, including vertical masonry walls and casemates. But at the same time cannon were gradually taken from the walls and shipped to Civil War battlefields. Then the war demonstrated that forts of this type could be destroyed from afar by the new rifled artillery. The improvements stopped in 1872. Some of the bastions remained sheathed in timber and no cannon were ever mounted in the casemates. After the war, three massive 15-inch Rodman guns, weighing 50,000 pounds each, were to be mounted on the bastion facing the lake. They arrived at the docks below the fort, remained stored there, and sometime after 1872 were shipped elsewhere.

In 1901 the fort was put briefly on caretaker status, but then as part of an overall army reorganization it became part of a battalion post for which new buildings were constructed in 1903-1905. The new post was built outside the fortifications, and for practical purposes they were abandoned. Fort Ontario continued as a military post through World War II, after which it became an emergency refuge center for victims of the Nazi Holocaust. In 1946 it was transferred to the State of New York and in 1949 became a State Historic Site.

Today the fortifications are largely restored to their condition as of 1870, the date by which most of the fort was completed. In the summer months uniformed interpreters perform ceremonies of the period and explain the fort to visitors. Within some of the buildings are exhibits that tell the story of the site from the French-and-Indian War to World War II. Outside the walls, graves in the post cemetery tell much the same story; among them is one of an officer of the Royal American Regiment and another of the King's Royal Regiment of New York, both of whom have been credited with being the ghost sometimes reported in the fort.

Fort Ontario, at Oswego, N.Y., is the best example of classic fort design in the Great Lakes area. This fort was built in 1839-1844 on the site of several earlier ones. It has been restored so that today it appears as it was about 1870. Air photo by B & D Photo Service, Oswego. (Fort Ontario State Historic Site)

PENETANGUISHENE, ST. JOSEPH, AND DRUMMOND

Three posts on Lake Huron or nearby waters were occupied by the British army as alternatives to Fort Mackinac. They were the fort on St. Joseph Island, about 40 miles from Mackinac, occupied from 1796 when the U.S. Army first took over Mackinac until the British recaptured it in 1812; the fort on Drummond Island (sometimes called Fort Collier because it was on Collier's Harbour, named after Captain Collier, the naval officer then in command on Lake Huron), closely adjoining St. Joseph but with a better harbor, occupied from 1815 when the British again left Mackinac until 1828, then abandoned because an unexpected quirk of the 1822 boundary survey had put it on the American side of the border; and Penetanguishene, where the soldiers moved in 1828 and remained until 1852. The latter station was placed on caretaker status until 1856 and then transferred to the provincial government (they soon turned it into a reformatory).

The first two of these forts are today in ruins, which in many ways conjure up the past as effectively as a restored fort, though in a different way. They leave more to the imagination, but we know that all of what we see is the original material. The fort at St. Joseph Island and the surrounding 800-acre park may be reached by car across a bridge from Sault Ste. Marie, Ontario. The fort at Drummond requires a ferry voyage from De Tour Village, Michigan; but failure in recent years to protect the site or to control development have erased or blocked access to most of the ruins at Drummond.

Penetanguishene (an Indian name said to mean "Place of the White Rolling Sands"), nearly two hundred miles to the southeast at the town of that name on Georgian Bay, is much more active today. It was an open post,

housing soldiers who guarded the backdoor approach to York (Toronto), which lies another hundred miles farther south. The stone barracks at the harbor mouth that would have given some protection in event of an attack have gone, but the stone officers' quarters remain and other buildings have been reconstructed. Archaeological work continues in the extensive area, and additional parts of it will eventually be opened to the public.

Penetanguishene was a naval base—its construction began during the War of 1812, was cancelled at the end of that war, then was

Old powder magazine on St. Joseph Island. (Photo by Robert Money)

The British forces on the western Great Lakes in 1828 withdrew to Georgian Bay, at Penetanguishene (an Indian name meaning "Place of the white rolling sand") where there already was a small naval base. At the reconstructed Naval and Military Establishment, Penetanguishene, schooners and smallboats of early nineteenth century pattern lie at the naval dock, where visitors can embark on short cruises. (Photo by the author)

restarted in 1817—before the army elements moved there from Drummond Island. One of its functions was as a logistical base for the post at Drummond, storing, guarding, and forwarding supplies. This made it the logical place for the troops to fall back on.

After the move, the combined base was known as the Naval & Military Establishments. In the nearby town, which grew up beside the Establishments, is the small garrison church of St. James-on-the-Lines, with a center aisle broad enough to admit soldiers marching in four abreast. The Establishments, which stretch for nearly a mile along the shore,

can be seen by walking tours (including evening tours by lantern light) or from horse-drawn "wagons" (actually, open busses) that carry visitors the length of the area. Uniformed interpreters carry out musket drill, but the emphasis is on the naval aspects of the history. There is a collection of rowing and sailing boats. Several schooners of early-nineteenth-century design, controlled by sailors in period costume but usually worked by adventurous visitors, provide an assortment of sailing experiences, from afternoon or sunset cruises to three-day programs for young people.

SAINTE MARIE AMONG THE HURONS

The fortified mission of Sainte Marie among the Hurons, the first European establishment on the Great Lakes, was burned by the French Jesuits in 1649 to keep it from being occupied by an invading Iroquois army. Those invaders drove out the Hurons, whose name for themselves was *Wendat,* and the fragments of whose nation became the Wyandots of later history in other places. Today the restored mission is at the original site, on the Wye River a short distance from Georgian Bay, near present-day Midland, Ontario.

Throughout the eighteenth and nineteenth centuries traders, explorers, and finally settlers frequently noted the location of the ruins. Thanks to the records left by the Jesuits, the story of Sainte Marie was well known, especially in French Canada, and so the significance of the crumbling walls and overgrown mounds of earth—which eventually lay undisturbed within a private hunting preserve—was always clear. In 1940 the land again came into the possession of the Jesuit Order. In the following years the Royal Ontario Museum and the University of Western Ontario conducted extensive archaeological digs which eventually led to reconstruction of the mission fort in wood and stone by the Ontario government. Archaeological work continues today.

Now a visitor can walk through the palisaded mission and see how the first Europeans existed in the wilderness, a month's canoe travel from Quebec, the nearest French base. The missionaries and their French workmen occupied the North Court and adjacent South Court work area of the mission. South of that was an area for Christian natives, called "a retreat for pilgrims." It contained the hospital and quarters such as the longhouse and wigwams that stand in the reconstructed mission today. Between inner and outer walls was an area for native guests who were not converts.

Visitors' pamphlets are available in a variety of languages, and guides who speak most of them are on call. Staff members play the parts of the priests and lay workmen who lived here and the Indians with whom they were in contact. Special children's programs are available. On particular evenings each week there are candlelight tours. Qualified guides lead canoe trips on the Wye river which flows past the fort. On the opposite side of the fort, just outside its walls, are a study center and library.

Some twenty miles northwest of Sainte Marie, on Christian Island—an Indian reservation now occupied by the Beausoleil First Nation—lie the ruins of Sainte Marie II. When the Jesuits burned the first Sainte Marie in 1649 to keep it from being occupied by the invading Iroquois, they and their French assistants, plus an undetermined number of Hurons (one estimate is as high as 8,000) moved first to Christian Island. There, on the sheltered bay along the southern shore of the island, the French built a small stone fort, 35 meters square with a bastion at each corner, to hold off further Iroquois attack. In 1650, after an agonizing winter during which there was no attack but many died from starvation and disease, the Jesuits and many of the Hurons left forever for Quebec.

The stone walls of the fort can still be seen. The locations of the European camp and of a Huron village of that winter are north of the fort, and other nearby areas continue to be excavated by archaeologists. The island can be reached by ferry from nearby Cedar Point.

Right: Inside the mission. (Photo by author)

Below: The oldest place on the Great Lakes inhabited by Europeans, the mission fort of Sainte Marie among the Hurons was built in 1644. This reconstruction, based on extensive archaeological work, has been built on the original site in recent years. The mission was defended on all sides by strong palisade walls. The pathway and railing along the river are modern embellishments. (Photo by author)

FORT WAYNE

Fort Wayne faces the Detroit River near Detroit's Fisher Freeway. The distance of only half-a-dozen blocks takes a driver from the rushing, roaring present of the motor city to the quiet, pre-automotive fort built in 1843-50. Among the city streets just off post are Infantry Street, Hussar Street, and Dragoon Street. The fort now belongs to the city of Detroit and because of financial problems it unfortunately is not open to the public at this writing.

The fort, named in 1849 after Anthony Wayne, was built as an earthen fort with timber revetments. As at Oswego, N.Y., where an improved Fort Ontario was built at about the same time, the fort was a response to the ticklish situation caused by a group of American activists—calling themselves Canadian "Patriots" though most of them had never been in Canada—who in this case gathered along the U.S. side of the Detroit River in order to mount an invasion of Canada. Perhaps two hundred of them were brave enough actually to invade Windsor and vicinity, but after some destruction and murder were met by a volley from a well-drilled company of Canadian militia, and fled in disorganized panic.

Aware that local politicians were strongly anti-Canadian, but trying hard to stave off future escapades that could cause a war, the federal government built Fort Wayne to seem an apparent gesture of defiance toward Canada and yet to give better control of the Detroit River shores if invaders again tried to gather there. But unlike the invaders from Oswego, who fought bravely if not too effectively, the swaggering pirates from Detroit would have been farcical if they were not also murderous. After their terrified retreat back to the U.S. side of the river they were scarcely heroes. Their public support dwindled away.

There also were enough troops in barracks in the city of Detroit to deter further invasions. Although the fort contains a handsome stone barracks constructed in 1848, troops remained in Detroit. Forts such as Wayne were normally manned by specialized artillery units, and the barracks remained empty awaiting one of them, though in the absence of further major problems with Canada none was ever assigned here. No cannon were ever mounted.

The fort was not occupied until 1861, when under the pressures of the Civil War it began to be used as a mustering post. The large garrison and the administrative and logistic functions of mobilization quickly moved outside the walls. In the area just outside the fortifications many white-painted frame buildings were put up to house the overflow. Fort Wayne, however, was perhaps the most extreme example of a fort that ran over its walls; here the overflow was so great that new buildings alone did not suffice, and sidewheel steamboats had to be tied up along the riverbank to provide extra quarters for the soldiers.

During and immediately after the Civil War the fort was updated. Inside the earthen outer defenses, it now is built of brick and stone, is square in shape, and has a bastion at each corner and a triangular projection called a demilune extending from the river side. If the fort had been prepared for battle, the demilune would have been the location for a battery of powerful artillery to command the river. It also gives added thickness to the most exposed wall of the fort. Flanking casemates (protected chambers within the walls, in this instance within the

Right: Completed in 1848 but not actually used until 1861, these stone barracks still stand as the center of Fort Wayne, Michigan, at Detroit. (Photo by author)

Below: Fort Wayne, at Detroit. The original 1848 barracks stand at left center. The square fort with diamond-shaped bastions at the corners was built in the late 1840s, then updated during and after the Civil War. In the left distance are some of the brick buildings of the large military post that developed outside the walls. (Historical Department, City of Detroit)

bastions) that would have allowed cannon to cover each wall with defensive fire were added in 1863.

Wartime tensions with Canada brought the Civil War improvements. Work on the fortifications continued into the 1870s. The war showed, however, that the new rifled artillery made masonry forts obsolete, and the work here ended, although the fortifications were still given reasonable upkeep and the space within them continued to be used. After that war the post became the home of a series of infantry regiments. A bridge or ramp was built over the walls, giving easy access from the open post outside to the area within the fort. Beginning in the 1880s the wooden structures were gradually replaced by brick ones.

The open post now has the brick structures of a typical pre-World War II army post—for example, ten comfortable duplexes built for families of noncommissioned officers—updated to become the major automotive supply center for the allied armies during World War II. It provides a clear cross-section of military life from the 1840s through World War II. Nearly all of the post, including the actual fort, was given to the city in 1949.

Below: Gate to the fortifications at Fort Wayne. It was cut through the walls in 1939, to permit vehicles to enter the fortifications and to give easier access from the post that had developed outside the fort. Inside the walls to the right is the 1848 barracks; in the distance is industrial Detroit. The cannon are decorative and would not have been fired from this position. (Photo by author)

Right: Officers' row in the military post outside the fort. (Photo by author)

Left: The commanding officers' house at Fort Wayne has been restored to its 1880s appearance. (Photo by author)

Right: Military posts that overflowed the original walls of some of the old fortifications were further developed and expanded as time passed. This post Guard House at Fort Wayne was built in 1905. (Photo by author)

FORT WILKINS

Fort Wilkins, a good example of a small frontier military post, has survived largely intact since its last garrison departed in 1870, and has required only moderate restoration to bring back its original flavor. It stands at Copper Harbor, on the tip of Michigan's Keweenaw Peninsula. Now the fort is the main attraction of the 199-acre Fort Wilkins State Park.

The Secretary of War, William Wilkins, established the fort in 1844. In 1846 the garrison was withdrawn at the outbreak of the Mexican War and the fort was put on caretaker status. It was regarrisoned in the 1860s at a time of increased stress with Canada, but the army left permanently in 1870.

The costumed staff portrays life as it was here in the 1800s. In the palisaded fort are quarters for enlisted men and officers, a powder magazine, a hospital, stores, mess halls, and other original buildings of the two-company post. It is typical of the many forts that were built along the frontiers to maintain peace among the Indians—and the frontiersmen—as the United States expanded. Many of them, like Fort Wilkins, served their purpose simply by being there and never saw any action.

Top Right: The rehabilitated Fort Wilkins as it now looks. (Michigan History Division)

Bottom Right: Fort Wilkins, Michigan, as it appears today. The water is that of a small lake, Lake Fanny Hooe (pronounced "hoe," like the garden tool). (Michigan History Division)

FORT WILLIAM

Old Fort William, largest fur-trade reconstruction in North America, is at Thunder Bay, Ontario on the Kaministiqua River, nine miles upstream from the point where the river flows into Lake Superior at the original Fort William site—which was overwhelmed by railway yards and grain elevators as civilization advanced. The actual fort was established when the North West Company moved their Lake Superior base here from Grand Portage in 1803; first it was called the New Fort, then in 1806 it became Fort William, named after the governor of the North West Company, William McGillivray.

The reconstructed fort at a new location takes visitors back to the days of the yearly "Great Rendezvous," when each July the North West Company partners from the interior met the partners from Montreal, deciding on the division of profits from the past year and the policies necessary for the coming one. At the same time, furs from the North and West were exchanged for trade goods brought out from Montreal. The voyageurs, clerks, and other employees of the company who gathered here each summer to carry out these jobs totaled about two thousand people. During the rendezvous, dances, feasts, and celebrations were interspersed with the pressing work.

There was a rendezvous each year from 1803 until 1821, when the North West Company merged with the Hudson's Bay Company. The fort then diminished in importance, but continued as a fur-trade post until it finally was closed in 1881. The Ontario government announced reconstruction of the post in 1971. The work, based on archaeological and documentary research, was enough completed by the summer of 1973 that the fort was opened to the public.

The reconstruction focuses on the year 1815, when the original fort was at its height. It is as complete as its namesake was, and many activities are carried out for visitors by trained artisans, guides, and interpreters. Within the palisaded fort are working craft shops—of the kind that maintained Fort William when it was alone in an isolated wilderness far from civilization—and there is a site for repair and construction of the large bark canoes used by the voyageurs. There are over forty buildings spread over twenty acres. Throughout the day, costumed interpreters can be seen as they press furs, saw logs, fire flintlock muskets, and prepare the foods of the period. Immediately adjacent to the fort is a farm of the same period, recreating one that was run by Jean-Marie Boucher, a semi-independant operator who supplied the fort with farm products.

Although the fort offers programs throughout the year, the largest event is a reenactment in July of the Great Rendezvous. It lasts about two weeks. Visitors come from far away, among them a group of American highland pipers, drummers, and dancers to help emphasize the Scottish background of the Nor'Westers, and organizations from Canada and the United States that recreate the arrival of Voyageurs.

Below: The eastern extremity of Old Fort William, as seen from the "observatory," or look-out tower. (Old Fort William)

Above The Great Hall at the reconstructed Fort William. (Old Fort William)

FORT YORK

Fort York is today in the middle of Toronto, with a freeway on one side and a railway yard on the other, and with the towers of the downtown city as a backdrop. (Only vigorous action by historic-minded people in the more recent past stopped in turn the railway, the freeway, and a developer from leveling the fort entirely.) Here a visitor can hardly escape the contrast between the early nineteenth-century fort and late twentieth-century civilization.

This fort recreates the 1816 fort that was built after three American thrusts during the war of 1812—the major one in April 1813, a small follow-up in July to make certain that the fort of that time was destroyed as completely as possible, and an even smaller, abortive naval reconnaissance in August that pulled back rather than attack the partly rebuilt fort. The fort that one sees now was built in an irregular shape that best fitted the terrain of the day. A straight wall faced the lake to the south (many years of landfill operations have moved the lakefront farther away, but originally Fort York stood on the shore of Lake Ontario). In the middle of this wall is a projecting half circle that housed the primary artillery battery of the fort. The heavy earthen walls were originally backed with wood, but during reconstruction stone was used instead. Some of the buildings are the original ones, some are reconstructions; in its relatively small area the fort could house 650 soldiers, though except in times of crisis there were usually 200-300.

The fort had much influence on the nearby growing town of York (now Toronto), where the inhabitants even set their clocks by the fort's noon gun, except for a while in 1825, "The sun dial at the Garrison west of this city has been eat up by one of His Majesty's Cows—The 12 o'clock gun is therefore fired by guesswork." In 1841 the garrison moved outside the walls into a new fort—barracks surrounded only by a palisade—but the old fort still provided the defensive position and during the tensions of the American Civil War a new seven-gun battery was emplaced along its southern wall, looking over the lake. When the British army left in 1870, the new fort became a Canadian military headquarters. Here was the historic post where in 1874 the first of the Northwest Mounted Police (now the Royal Canadian Mounted Police) were recruited and trained. Although the old fort remained government ground and was used occasionally for military exercises, the fortifications gradually fell into disrepair.

Restoration of the old fort began in 1934. During World War II the fort deteriorated, but in 1949 restoration began again. In the 1940s the less dramatic "New Fort"—which in 1893 had been renamed Stanley Barracks after Lord Stanley, then Governor General of Canada— lost its own struggle for survival, was swallowed up by the grounds of the annual Canadian National Exhibition, and six of its seven original buildings were destroyed. (Its single remaining building, the old officers' quarters, now houses a marine museum, though within the museum there also is one room where visitors with advance reservations can attend an 1893 officers' mess ten-course dinner party, with uniformed actors playing appropriate parts.)

But in the complete, restored 1816 fort, staff members in costumes of that day take the roles of the women who cooked in the kitchen and of the British soldiers who drilled on the parade ground to fife and drum. The officers' quarters here have authentic furnishings. There is a restored barrack room. The visitor can readily observe these things, at the same time looking beyond the walls and savoring the contrast between past and present.

Top: The original officers' quarters at Fort York. (Photo by the author)

Bottom: Fort York against the background of modern Toronto. (Photo by the author)

RUINS, RESTORATION, AND RECONSTRUCTION

Previous Page Top: On St. Joseph Island are the ruins of the British post there which was maintained from the time the British relinquished Fort Mackinac to the Americans after the Revolution until they recaptured Mackinac at the beginning of the War of 1812. These probably were administrative buildings. (Photo by Robert Money)

Previous Page Bottom: At Heritage Hill State Park, Green Bay, Wisconsin, several buildings of Fort Howard are preserved. Here the Fort Howard Hospital is being restored. It was built in 1834 and after the fort closed was located in several places around Green Bay, since 1929 as a museum. In 1975 it was moved to Heritage Hill. It is used to display and explain medical techniques of the Fort Howard era. (Heritage Hill)

Above: The reconstructed Fort William as seen today. (Old Fort William)

Bottom: A bateau with costumed passengers arrives for the re-creation of the yearly Great Rendezvous, held each July. (Old Fort William)

ACKNOWLEDGEMENTS

I am much indebted to many people for help in gathering information and illustrations for this book.

Foremost among them is Prof. William Money of Lake Superior State University, who took many photos of the remaining military buildings and ruins in the Sault Ste. Marie area, found old photos of Fort Brady, and offered much encouragement in the early days of my researches. Particular thanks go also to Dr. William Phenix, who strongly supported the book, who permitted me to visit and photograph Fort Wayne although that post was closed to the public, and who provided the air photo of the fort.

The late B.C. Morse, Jr., who was born at Fort Mackinac, kindly provided family photographs, discussed his early days at the fort, and gave enthusiastic encouragement for the book.

Kenn Knapman provided the picture of Oswego c. 1760 from his private collection and showed much interest in the work.

The gracious and helpful people at the National Archives of Canada are too numerous to list, but they were a major source of assistance.

Thanks indeed for information, illustrations, and encouragement to Mark Bollinger, Grand Portage; D. Wayne Campbell, Travelpic Publications; Ron Dale, Fort George; Bob Garcia, Fort Malden; Marcelle Karner, Heritage Hill State Park (Fort Howard); Kimberley MacLennan, Parks of the St. Lawrence (Fort Henry); Marty Mascarin, Fort William; Judy Ann Miller, Mackinac State Historical Parks; Judy Saunders, Fort Erie; and Patrick A. Wilder, Fort Ontario.

And to the many others who eased my way, my heartfelt gratitude.

Soo, Mich. Troops at Fort Brady, Standing Inspection.

Left: The plan of the first Fort Brady, 1822. (One building at the top left had burned.) The buildings were surrounded by a palisade. There were two block-houses, one at each of the opposing corners of the rectangle. (U.S. National Archives, RG 77, Fort File, Dr. 1-2)

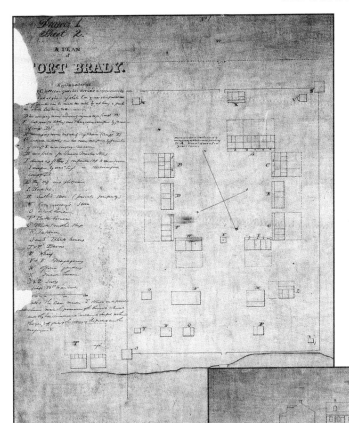

Right: At Fort Brady, in addition to the cantonment there were a number of other buildings inside the palisade, including a hospital, a commissary, a blacksmith shop, and a school house. (U.S. National Archives, RG 77, Fort File, Dr. 1-2)

Previous Page: At "New" Fort Brady, soldiers stand full field inspection in the field uniform of the Spanish-American War period. The buildings in the background are today part of Lake Superior State University. (Lake Superior State University)

A NOTE ON TERMINOLOGY

Many technical engineering terms apply to forts and their various features. Most of them have been avoided here, but a few are essential.

BASTION. A structure built where two walls meet and so arranged that the defenders can fire from it along the walls at any attackers. In formally planned forts, such as Fort Ontario, a bastion, seen from a height, is usually a diamond-shaped structure partly embedded in the wall and projecting from it.

BATTERY. A set of cannon, defined by their location ("the west battery" or "the forward battery" at Fort Henry), or by the organization of soldiers that man them ("Battery A"). By extension, a battery can also be the place where guns are to be located in the future or have been located in the past ("The Battery" in New York City). Field batteries, consisting of mobile cannon used outside the forts, were often named for the battery commanders ("Biddle's Battery" and "Ritchie's Battery" at the Battle of Chippewa).

CASEMATE. A chamber built within the walls of a fort. Casemates can house barracks, guardhouse, mess hall, and other administrative functions that otherwise would require separate buildings. Fort Henry is an example of a fort with such casemates. Casemates also furnish positions from which cannon and small arms can be fired at an attacker through ports or embrasures in the walls. In the American forts that have them—Niagara, Ontario, Wayne—they are intended for this purpose.

DRY DITCH or **DRY MOAT.** A ditch that surrounds the walls of a fort, hindering any attacker and giving an open area into which guns of the fort may fire. In Fort Henry, which lacks bastions, the dry ditch is especially important; weapons are sited to fire along it and thus serve the same purpose as bastions.

EMBRASURE. A small opening in a wall through which weapons may be fired.

GUARDHOUSE. A building, casemate, or group of rooms housing the guard of the day and any prisoners. It may also have offices for the Provost Officer or Provost Sergeant in charge of the prisoners, and sometimes for other officers. The guard of the day is a group of soldiers assigned to the guard for a 24 hour period. Usually it is divided into three reliefs which rotate, so that one is always on guard duty during the period, the other two off duty but on call, probably asleep in the guardhouse. During peacetime the prisoners kept in the guardhouse are usually those members of the garrison serving short sentences for minor infractions; serious criminals go to federal prisons.

LUNETTE and **DEMILUNE.** A lunette is a V-shaped defensive structure pointing outward. A lunette is part of the outer works at the southeastern corner of Fort Niagara. A demilune, as the name implies, is a smaller version. The demilune at Fort Wayne is a V-shaped projection on the most exposed side of the fort; a powerful artillery battery was to be mounted on it.

MAGAZINE. The structure where kegs of gunpowder, and in later years more sophisticated munitions, are stored. It can be a casemate or a separate building. It may also contain weapons.

PALISADE or **STOCKADE.** A barrier of sharpened logs closely planted in the earth. The logs can be vertical or can project horizontally from earthworks.

RAVELIN. A large, V-shaped outerwork (usually outside the dry ditch) that protects the gate or other weak point in a fort. The one at Fort Erie, for example, protects the gate from a landing by water.

REDOUBT. The word is sufficiently broad to give confusion. It has two basic meanings. In the first, it refers to small defensive works such as blockhouses or minor earthworks that are located by themselves, away from other fortifications. In the second, it refers to detached works that are part of a larger defensive plan. Most commonly, as at Fort Erie, such redoubts are V-shaped structures located outside the walls of a fort to add to its defenses; the open end of the V is toward the fort, so that if the redoubt is captured it can be swept by fire from the fort and is of no use to the attacker. But the term is also used for the free-standing towers inside the walls of Fort Niagara. It even has been applied to the massive Fort Henry because that fort was built without bastions and in the early planning was to have its walls covered by fire from other nearby fortifications that were never built. But when Henry was constructed, military engineers were beginning to omit bastions from new forts. It was designed so that it could cover its own walls quite effectively, and it is hard to imagine a force that could have taken Henry by direct assault.

REVETMENT. A facing of wood or masonry to retain an earthwork.

SALLY PORT. A gate through which soldiers can sally forth to counterattack the enemy. In larger forts it usually includes a tunnel through the walls.

STAR FORT. A fort with no bastions, but with jagged walls. Usually quite small. Seen from above, the walls suggest the outline of a conventionalized star. Fort Mississauga is a star fort. Fort Ontario, though sometimes given that description because of its pointed bastions, is not.

SELECTED BIBLIOGRAPHY

References dealing with the history of the Great Lakes region, and at least incidentally with the forts there and the reasons for building them, are so numerous that a complete list would fill a volume of its own. The following are suggested as background.

GENERAL

Barry, James P. "U.S. - Canadian Frictions Along the Great Lakes - St. Lawrence Border." *Inland Seas* . Vol 45, 1989.

Beers, Henry Putney. *The French and British in the Old Northwest.* Detroit: Wayne State University Press, 1964. [Condensed history and guide to sources.]

Bowler, R. Arthur. *War Along the Niagara.* Youngstown, N.Y.: Old Fort Niagara Association, 1991.

Caruso, John Anthony. *The Great Lakes Frontier.* Indianapolis and New York: Bobbs-Merrill Company, 1961.

Champlain, Samuel de. *The Works of Samuel de Champlain.* 6 vols. Edited by H.P. Biggar. Toronto: The Champlain Society, 1922-36.

Cranston, J.H. *Etienne Brûlé, Immortal Scoundral.* Toronto: The Ryerson Press, 1949.

Cruickshank, E.A. (ed.) *Letters and Papers of John Graves Simcoe.* 5 vols. Toronto: Ontario Historical Society, 1923-31.

Cuthbertson, George A. *Freshwater.* Toronto: The Macmillan Company of Canada, 1931.

De Voto, Bernard. *The Course of Empire.* Boston: Houghton Mifflin Company, 1952.

Edmunds, R. David. *The Shawnee Prophet.* Lincoln: University of Nebraska Press, 1983.

Fridley, Russell W. and Holmquist, June Drenning (eds.). *Aspects of the Fur Trade.* St. Paul: Minnesota Historical Society, 1967.

Fryer, Mary Beacock. *King's Men: The Soldier Founders of Ontario.* Toronto: Dundurn Press, 1980.

Heriot, George. *Travels Through the Canadas.* London: Richard Phillips, 1807.

Hickey, Donald R. *The War of 1812: A Forgotten Conflict.* Urbana and Chicago: University of Illinois Press, 1989.

Hitsman, J. Mackay. *The INCREDIBLE War of 1812.* Toronto: University of Toronto Press, 1965.

Innis, Harold A. *The Fur Trade in Canada.* New Haven: Yale University Press, 1962.

Jacobs, James Ripley. *The Beginning of the U.S. Army, 1783-1812.* Princeton: Princeton University Press, 1947.

Jaenen, Cornelius J. *Friend and Foe.* Toronto: McClelland and Stewart, 1976.

Kilbourn, William. *The Firebrand: William Lyon Mackenzie and the Rebellion in Upper Canada.* Toronto and Vancouver: Clarke Irwin & Co., 1956.

Knopf, Richard C. *Anthony Wayne and the Founding of the United States Army.* Columbus: Anthony Wayne Parkway Board, Ohio Historical Center, 1961.

Landon, Fred. *Western Ontario and the American Frontier.* New Haven: Yale University Press, 1941.

Lavender, David. *The Fist in the Wilderness.* Garden City, N.Y. : Doubleday & Company, 1964.

Lewis, Emanuel Raymond. *Seacoast Fortifications of the United States.* Seventh printing, with corrections. Annapolis, Maryland: Naval Institute Press, 1993. [No specific Great Lakes information, but much background.]

Lossing, Benson. *Pictorial Field-Book of the War of 1812.* New York: Harper & Brothers, 1868.

MacKay, Douglas. *The Honourable Company.* Indianapolis and New York: The Bobbs-Merrill Company, 1936.

Newman, Peter C. *Company of Adventurers.* Markham, Ontario: Penguin Books Canada, 1985.

_____. *Caesars of the Wilderness.* Markham, Ontario: Penguin Books Canada, 1987.

Pound, Arthur. *Johnson of the Mohawks.* New York: The Macmillan Company, 1930.

_____. *Lake Ontario.* Indianapolis and New York: The Bobbs-Merrill Company, 1945.

Prucha, Francis Paul (ed.). *Army Life on the Western Frontier.* Selections from the Official Reports Made Between 1826 and 1845 by Colonel George Croghan. Norman: University of Oklahoma Press, 1958.

Quaife, Milo M. (ed.). *Alexander Henry's Travels and Adventures.* Chicago: The Lakeside Press, 1921.

_____ . (ed.). *The John Askin Papers.* 2 vols. Detroit Library Commission, 1928.

_____ . *Lake Michigan.* Indianapolis and New York: The Bobbs-Merrill Company, 1944.

Sandoz, Mari. *The Beaver Men .* New York: Hastings House, 1964.

Severance, Frank A. *An Old Frontier of France.* 2 vols. New York: Dodd, Mead and Company, 1917.

Stanley, George F.G. and Preston, Richard A. *A Short History of Kingston as a Military and Naval Centre.* Kingston, Ontario: Department of History, Royal Military College, 1950.

Thwaites, Reuben Gold (ed.). *The Jesuit Relations* . Vols 5-8, 10, 12. Cleveland: Burrows Brothers, 1896-1901,

_____ (ed.). *Lahontan's Voyages to North America.* 2 vols. Reprinted from English edition of 1703. Chicago. A.C. McClurg & Co., 1905.

Voorhis, Ernest. *Historical Forts and Trading Posts of the French Regime and of the English Fur Trading Companies.* Ottawa: Department of the Interior, 1930.

Welsh, William Jeffrey and Skaggs, David Curtis (eds.) *War on the Great Lakes.* Kent, Ohio: The Kent State University Press, 1991. [Battles of Lake Erie and Thames; bibliographic guide.]

Wittke, Carl. "Ohioans and the Canadian American Crisis of 1837-38," *The Ohio State Archaeological and Historical Quarterly.* Vol 58, 1949.

References to Specific Forts

Barry, James P. "When Fort Niagara Fell." *American History Illustrated* . May 1968.

_____ . *Georgian Bay: The Sixth Great Lake.* Revised ed. Toronto and Vancouver: Clarke, Irwin & Company, 1968. [Ste. Marie, Penetanguishene]

_____ . *Georgian Bay: An Illustrated History.* Toronto: Stoddart,1992. [Ste. Marie, Penetanguishene]

Benn, Carl. *Historic Fort York, 1793-1993.* Toronto: Natural Heritage/Natural History, 1993.

Bradford, Robert D. *Historic Forts of Ontario.* Belleville, Ontario: Mika Publishing Company, 1988.

Cruikshank, Lieut.-Colonel Ernest. *The Battle of Fort George.* Niagara-on-the-Lake, Ontario: Niagara Historical Society, 1990.

Detroit Historical Commission. *Historic Fort Wayne.* Detroit: n.d.

Detroit Historical Museum. *Cadillac's Village: Detroit under the French Regime.* Detroit: 1958.

Dunnigan, Brian Leigh. *The British Army at Mackinac, 1812-1815.* Reports in Mackinac History and Archaeology no. 7. Mackinac Island: Mackinac Island State Park Commission, 1980.

_____. *Glorious Old Relic: The French Castle and Old Fort Niagara.* Youngstown, N.Y.: Old Fort Niagara Association, 1987.

_____. *Forts Within a Fort: Niagara Redoubts.* Youngstown, N.Y.: Old Fort Niagara Association, 1989.

Dunnigan, Brian Leigh and Scott, Patricia Kay. *Old Fort Niagara in Four Centuries: A History of Its Development.* Youngstown, N.Y.: Old Fort Niagara Association, 1991.

Grant, W.L. "The Capture of Oswego by Montcalm." *Proceedings of the Royal Society of Canada.* Vol 2, 1914.

Harmon, Daniel Williams. *A Journal of Voyages and Travels in the Interior of North America* Andover: Flagg and Gould, 1820. [Grand Portage and Fort William.]

Havighurst, Walter. *Three Flags at the Straits: The Forts of Mackinac.* Englewood Cliffs, N.J.: Prentice-Hall, 1966.

Heidenreich, Conrad. *Huronia.* Toronto: McClelland and Stewart, 1971. [Ste. Marie.]

Heritage Hill State Park. Papers on history of Fort Howard. Green Bay, Wisconsin: n.d.

Jury, Elsie McLeod and Jury, Wilfred. *The Establishments at Penetanguishene.* London, Ont.: Museum of Indian Archaeology, University of Western Ontario, 1959.

Jury, Wildred and Jury, Elsie McLeod. *Sainte-Marie among the Hurons.* Toronto: Oxford University Press, 1954.

Lindley, Harlow (ed.). *Fort Meigs and the War of 1812: Orderly Book of Cushing's Company and Personal Diary of Captain Daniel Cushing.* Columbus: The Ohio Historical Society, 1975.

Litt, Paul; Williamson, Ronald F.; and Whitehorne, Joseph W.A. *Death at Snake Hill: Secrets From a War of 1812 Cemetery.* Ontario Heritage Foundation Local History Series No. 3. Toronto & Oxford: Dundurn Press, 1993. [Fort Erie.]

Lumby, John R. *Historic Fort William.* 1927. Reprint. Belleville, Ontario: Mika Publishing, 1974.

Mason, Philip P. *Detroit, Fort Lernoult, and the American Revolution.* Detroit: Wayne State University Press, 1964.

Michigan Department of State. *Fort Wilkins Historic Complex.* Lansing: n.d.

Old Fort Niagara Association. *A History and Guide to Old Fort Niagara.* Youngstown, N.Y.: 1990.

Peterson, Eugene T. *Mackinac Island: Its History in Pictures.* Mackinac Island: Mackinac Island State Park Commission, 1973.

Phenix, William P. "Never a Shot in Anger." *Michigan History*. Vol. 65, No. 3, May/June 1981. [Fort Wayne.]

_____. "Restoration: More Than a Coat of Paint." *Michigan History*. Vol 65, No. 3, May/June 1981. [Fort Wayne.]

Porter, Phil. *The Eagle at Mackinac: The Establishment of United States Military and Civil Authority on Mackinac Island 1796-1802*. Reports in Mackinac History and Archaeology Number 11. Mackinac Island: Mackinac State Historic Parks, 1991.

Pouchot, Pierre. *Memoir upon the late War in North America*. Translated and edited by Franklin B. Hough. Roxbury, Mass.: W.E. Woodward, 1866. [Fort Niagara.]

Saint Lawrence Parks Commission. *Old Fort Henry*. Kingston, Ontario: Fort Henry, n.d.

Smith, William Henry. "The Pelham Papers—Loss of Oswego." *Papers of the American Historical Association*. Vol 4, Part 4, 1890.

Stacey, Colonel C.P. *The Battle of Little York*. Toronto: Toronto Historical Board, 1971.

Thompson, Erwin N. *Grand Portage: A History of the Sites, People, and Fur Trade*. Washington: U.S. Department of the Interior, National Park Service, 1969. [Also much general fur-trade information and fur-trade bibliography.]

_____. *Grand Portage Monument Great Hall*. Washington: U.S. Department of the Interior, National Park Service, 1970. [Much on life at Grand Portage and other fur-trade posts.]

Wallace, W. Stewart. "Fort William of the Fur Trade." *The Beaver*. December 1949.

Whitehorne, Joseph W.A. *While Washington Burned: The Battle for Fort Erie 1814*. Baltimore: The Nautical & Aviation Publishing Company of America, 1992.

Widder, Keith R. *Reveille till Taps*. Mackinac Island: Mackinac Island State Park Commission, 1972.

Wood, Bvt. Lieut-Colonel Eleazer D. *Journal of the Northwestern Campaign of 1812-1813*. Defiance, Ohio: The Defiance College Press, 1975. [Fort Meigs]

Woodford, Frank B. and Woodford, Arthur M. *All Our Yesterdays*. Detroit: Wayne State University Press, 1969. [Fort Wayne, Michigan]

Woolworth, Nancy L. "Grand Portage in the Revolutionary War," *Minnesota History*. Summer, 1975.

Workmaster, Wallace F. "The Forts of Oswego: A Study in the Art of Defense." *Northeast Historical Archaeology*. Spring, 1972.

The British garrison stationed at Drummond Island moved to Penetanguishene in 1828. Stone barracks to house it were placed so as also to defend the narrow entrance to the harbor. In this 1836 painting by G. R. Dartnell, looking south in Penetanguishene Bay, the barracks are in the left distance and the remainder of the Naval and Military Establishment lies along the shore beyond them. (Royal Ontario Museum 952.87.5/69 Can 17)

INDEX

Page numbers in bold type indicate a photo or picture reference.

Naval and Military Establishment, Penetanguishene, at the southern end of Georgian Bay, 1818. The post was begun by the British during the War of 1812, but not finally established until 1817. It was primarily a naval base, though there was also a small military force. One of its functions was to store, guard, and transport supplies to the British post at Drummond Island. The protective stockades were around the base headquarters at left, and the naval storehouse, at right. The schooner in center foreground is the *Confiance*–the former U.S. schooner *Scorpion*–captured near Mackinac in 1814. (Metropolitan Toronto Reference Library, J. Ross Robertson Collection, T-16591)

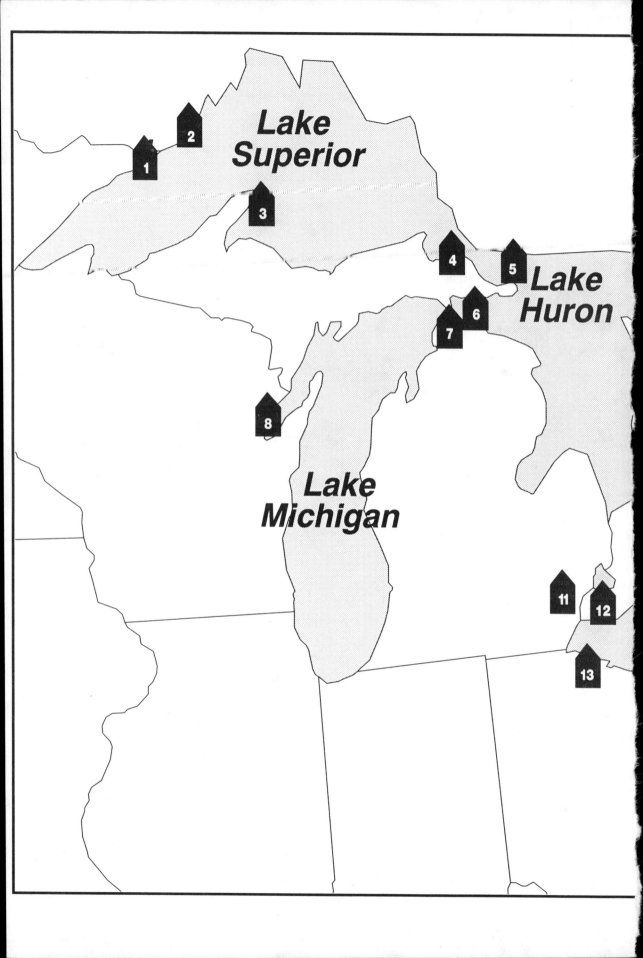